PAT BROWN, MBA

Financial Literacy For NIL

The Student-Athlete's Guide to Money, Branding, and Building Wealth in the NIL Era

ABRAM 47 BROWN

First published by AbramBrown47 2025

First edition

ISBN: 978-1-967737-00-0

This book was professionally typeset on Reedsy.
Find out more at reedsy.com

Contents

Preface

Let's get one thing straight: I wrote this book partly because I'm still a little salty.

When I was playing football at the University of Kansas, NIL wasn't even a whisper. If you even *looked* at a free meal sideways, someone from compliance might come running. Today's athletes, on the other hand, are out here building personal brands, launching businesses, and securing endorsement deals—and I love that for them. Seriously. But also... I would've crushed it.

So yes, I'm a little bitter—but mostly, I'm motivated.

This book, *Financial Literacy For NIL,* was born out of experience and a calling. I know firsthand what it feels like to be a student-athlete who's passionate, talented, and driven—but financially unprepared. I came from a loving home, but we didn't talk about money around the dinner table. I didn't know about taxes, budgeting, or credit. I had no clue how to build wealth or protect it. I had dreams, but no road map.

Then I took a financial literacy class specifically designed for athletes, and I realized just how much I didn't know. That moment was humbling—but it lit a fire in me. I knew I had to close that gap, not just for myself, but for every athlete coming up behind me.

This book is for them—and it's also for the people who shaped me.

First and foremost, I dedicate this book to my mother, **Drema Brown**, who passed away in 2024. My mother was my biggest cheerleader and greatest encourager. She always told me I could do anything I put my mind to, and that a positive attitude would carry me further than talent ever could. Her love and belief in me still guide every step I take. Mom, this book—and the mission behind it—is because of you.

To my wife, **Cassandra**—thank you for your unwavering support in everything I do. No matter what vision I bring to the table, you're there—encouraging me, standing beside me, and believing in me. Your strength and faith in my journey have helped carry me through every chapter.

To our daughters, **Peyton** and **Ryan**—you are my greatest source of pride and purpose. Peyton, watching you graduate from USC in Los Angeles and go on to earn your master's degree filled me with overwhelming joy. Ryan, your creativity and commitment led you to graduate from the Fashion Institute of Technology (F.I.T.) in New York City—and you've inspired me every step of the way. Everything I teach, everything I build—I hope it makes your paths just a little smoother and your futures a lot brighter.

To my father, **Timothy Brown Sr.**, a quiet Marine whose actions always spoke louder than words—thank you for showing me what it means to be strong, loyal, and disciplined. You taught me to finish what I start, even when it gets hard—and that lesson has stayed with me for life.

To my brother, **Timothy Brown II**, thank you for taking me with you to every court and gym when we were kids. Playing pickup games against older, stronger players gave me the grit, toughness, and confidence I carried onto the field and now into my professional life. I wouldn't be the competitor I am without those early lessons.

This book is also part of something bigger—a mission to make financial education accessible to athletes, families, and professionals across the board. That mission has led to the creation of several platforms, each one designed to provide real-world knowledge in a practical, approachable way:

- **www.FinancialLiteracyForNIL.com** – A hub for navigating NIL contracts, taxes, branding, and long-term financial planning.
- **www.FinancialLiteracyForStudentAthletes.com** – Covering budgeting, saving, credit, and life skills every young athlete should know.
- **www.FinancialLiteracyForCollegeCoaches.com** – Helping coaches become better mentors off the field.
- **www.ParentsOfStudentAthletes.com** – Empowering parents to

support their children's financial journey.

- **www.FinancialLiteracyForProAthletes.com** – Providing guidance for athletes turning pro so they don't just get rich—they stay rich.
- And expanding into broader professional and cultural spaces:
- **www.FinancialLiteracyForDoctors.com**
- **www.FinancialLiteracyForAttorneys.com**
- **www.FinancialLiteracyForTheCulture.com**
-

Each of these platforms reflects the same vision as this book: to give people the knowledge and tools they need to win beyond the game.

So no, I didn't get to cash in on NIL. But maybe I wasn't supposed to. Maybe my purpose was to help you—today's athletes—make the most of the opportunity I never had.

This is your time. Your playbook. Your future.

Let's build something that lasts.

— Pat Brown, MBA

NIL has changed the rules—but no one wins without a playbook.

Think about your sport. Would you ever step onto the field or court without knowing the playbook? Would you try to compete in a high-stakes game without knowing the rules, the strategies, or the responsibilities of your position? Of course not. That would be reckless—and it would cost you.

Now apply that same logic to your finances.

Name, Image, and Likeness (NIL) has unlocked doors that generations of college athletes never had access to. You can now earn money from your talent, your brand, your hustle, and your personality—all while still a student. It's empowering. It's exciting. It's long overdue.

But it's also dangerous if you're not prepared.

Because while the game has changed, too many student-athletes are being thrown into this new financial world without a playbook. Deals are being signed without understanding the fine print. Taxes are being ignored. Budgets are non-existent. Money is being spent faster than it's coming in. The truth is, money without knowledge is a setup for disaster.

Let's call it what it is: NIL is a business. That makes you a business owner. You've now got income, responsibilities, risks, and—if you do it right—real long-term opportunity. But like any business, success depends on how well you manage what's coming in and going out. It depends on how well you plan, protect, and grow what you've earned.

That's why you need this playbook.

This book isn't just going to throw financial jargon at you. It's written in your language, with real-life examples and sports analogies that actually make sense. We're going to talk about budgeting like it's your game plan, investing like it's your training program, taxes like they're the referees, and financial pressure like it's your toughest opponent. And just like you'd never trust a coach who doesn't know the game, you shouldn't trust financial advice from people who aren't qualified—no offense to your uncle who teaches seventh-grade math.

This book will teach you how to ask the right questions, spot red flags, and build a trusted team around you—CPAs, financial advisors, agents—people like myself, Pat Brown, MBA, who understand what it means to protect and grow your NIL potential.

We'll also talk about the long game. Because NIL is not forever. You might go pro, you might not. You might get injured, you might change careers. But what you do with your NIL money now—how you manage it, invest it, protect it—can determine whether you're still benefiting from it twenty years down the road.

NIL is here. The money is real. The opportunities are incredible. But without a financial game plan, you're just freelancing. And in every sport, we know how that ends.

This book helps you handle money, make smart choices, and plan for "the current you" and "the future you.

Let's break that down.

The *current you* is living in the moment—balancing classes, practices, games, workouts, social life, and, now, NIL opportunities. You're getting exposure. You're making moves. You may be earning money for the first time in your life. And with that money comes a lot of choices: What should I buy? Who should I help? How do I make it last?

The *future you*? That version of you is a little quieter right now, but it's counting on you to make good decisions today. The future you is the person you'll be five, ten, even thirty years from now. The one who wants to be financially secure. The one who wants to own property, start a business, take care of your family, give back to your community—or simply have options.

This book is about making sure both versions of you win.

So many student-athletes focus only on the now—and it makes sense. You're under a lot of pressure. You're trying to keep up with school, teammates, fans, expectations, and maybe even a few haters. There's not always time to think about retirement when you're just trying to make it through the week. But that's where the trap lies.

Money isn't just about what it can buy you today. It's about what it can *do for you* long after the lights go off and the crowd stops cheering. If you can be disciplined with your decisions now, you give the future you a head start that most people only dream of.

What would it look like if you saved just 20% of your NIL income and invested it wisely? What if you had a tax plan so you didn't get blindsided by the IRS next year? What if you talked to a financial advisor who actually cared about your long-term success and not just the next commission?

Too often, athletes are reactive with money. This book is about helping you become proactive.

You'll learn how to create a budget that works for your lifestyle—not something restrictive, but something real. You'll understand how credit works, why your credit score matters, and how to build it up. You'll learn how to evaluate NIL deals and avoid the ones that might look good upfront but hurt you later. You'll get the basics of investing, so your money can grow while you sleep. And you'll discover how insurance, legal protection, and smart partnerships can protect what you're building.

Everything in this book is designed to help you manage the *now* while building toward the *next*. Because the truth is, the current you deserves to enjoy this moment—and the future you deserves to benefit from it, too.

So whether you're cashing your first NIL check or just starting to build your brand, this book has your back. You don't need to be perfect—you just need to be prepared.

Featuring insights and guidance from Pat Brown, MBA—former D1 football player and trusted financial advocate for student-athletes nationwide.

How to Use This Book

Let's get something straight right off the bat — this book isn't here to lecture you. It's not a textbook, it's not a school assignment, and nobody's checking to see if you read every chapter or underline every sentence.

This book is a reference guide. A resource. A financial literacy playbook (yes, pun intended). **Feel free to write all over this book, make notes, make reminders!**

It was written for student-athletes like you — people who are navigating the new world of NIL, money, decisions, opportunities, and potential pitfalls — all while trying to balance school, sports, and real life. I know that your time is limited, your schedule is packed, and you've already got people pulling at you from every direction.

So here's the good news: you don't have to read this whole book all at once.

In fact, you don't even have to read it in order. Start with the table of contents. Take a look at the topics. You might see a chapter on budgeting and think, *"I already know that stuff."* Cool — skip it (or skim it). But maybe the chapter on taxes hits a little different. Or maybe you just got offered a brand deal and now you're wondering, *"Do I need an agent? A lawyer? A financial advisor? What do these people actually do?"* That's your entry point. Go straight there.

This book is meant to grow with you. You might read one chapter now and another three months from now. You might highlight something today and not fully understand it until your second NIL season. That's okay. That's how this works.

The goal isn't to make you an expert overnight. The goal is exposure — exposing you to the ideas, terms, and concepts that will help you build a strong financial foundation. Even if you don't fully grasp something right away, you'll at least know the topic exists — and that gives you a huge advantage. Because when you know what questions to ask, you're less likely to get taken advantage of.

Keep This Book Close

Don't treat this like some book you toss in your locker and forget. Keep it in your backpack, your dorm, or wherever you can access it easily. Think of it like a tool. You might not need it every day, but when something pops up — a new NIL deal, a credit issue, a conversation about investing — you'll have a place to turn.

Use this book when:

- You're about to make a money decision and want to understand your options
- You hear a financial term you don't know and want a quick breakdown
- You're working with a CPA, advisor, or agent and want to ask smarter questions
- You just want to level up your game off the field

Whether you're the type to sit down and binge a whole book in one weekend or you'd rather pick it up one chapter at a time during a bus ride or after practice — do what works for you.

Because this journey? It's yours. This money? It's yours. And the future you're building — it starts with knowing how the game is played.

So flip the page, jump around, come back later — whatever you need. Just know that this playbook was written for *you*. Let's run the right plays.

You ready? Let's go.

Let me formally introduce myself..

I'm Pat Brown. I played Division I football at the University of Kansas in the mid-to-late '90s, where I had the honor of serving as a team captain. After college, I continued my athletic journey in the CFL, playing for the Calgary Stampeders. I know firsthand what it means to be a student-athlete—the early mornings, the late nights, the pressure to perform on and off the field. I've felt the weight of expectation. I've lived the discipline. And like so many others, I also learned what it felt like to be under prepared when it came to money.

See, no one ever sat me down to talk about financial literacy when I was a student-athlete. We talked about schemes, opponents, and game film. But not once did anyone teach me how to read a credit report, file taxes, open an investment account, or prepare for life after the game.

And honestly? I was embarrassed. Embarrassed that I didn't know how money worked. Embarrassed that I didn't ask the questions I should have. And even more embarrassed when I realized that financial education wasn't just lacking for me—it was missing for almost every student-athlete I knew, especially those who looked like me or came from communities where money wasn't openly discussed at the dinner table.

That experience drove me to study finance, earn my MBA, and become a licensed financial advisor. Today, I work every day to bridge the gap between athletic talent and financial understanding. I've spent over 20 years helping individuals, families, and, most importantly, student-athletes build financial foundations that last beyond the game.

I created platforms like **Financial Literacy for NIL**, **Financial Literacy for Student-Athletes**, Financial **Literacy for College Coaches** and **Financial Literacy for the Culture** to make sure no athlete has to guess their way through these life-changing moments. I've spoken at universities, hospitals, churches, and community events, always with the same mission: to empower young people with the tools and mindset they need to thrive.

Because here's the truth—talent can open doors, but financial literacy will determine whether you can walk through them and stay there. NIL is a powerful opportunity, but it also brings risk. The decisions you make now can either set you up for long-term peace or long-term pain. I've seen both. And that's why this book exists.

This isn't theory. This is real-life guidance from someone who's been in your cleats. I know the culture, the mindset, and the blind spots. And I'm here to help you navigate it all.

So as you move through these pages, know that you're not alone. I've been where you are. And now, it's my mission to help you go further than you ever thought possible—on and off the field.

Quick Note..

Let me be clear right from the jump—I'm not a writer, and I'm definitely not trying to pretend to be one. This book isn't going to follow all the formal rules of grammar, structure, or what some people might call "proper book etiquette." You might catch a typo, a run-on sentence, or something that makes an English teacher cringe. And you know what? That's okay.

This isn't about being perfect. It's about being real.

I wrote this book because I've got a message that needs to be heard. Too many student-athletes are stepping into a new world of money, deals, and decisions—and they're doing it without the tools they need to succeed. That's why this book exists.

So if the wording gets a little rough or the grammar isn't textbook, I hope you'll give me some grace and stay focused on what matters most: the information, the message, and the mission.

Thanks for reading—and more importantly, thanks for taking your financial future seriously.

The New Game: NIL and the Modern Athlete

Welcome to a new era in college sports.

For the first time in history, student-athletes are finally able to profit from their **Name, Image, and Likeness (NIL)**. Whether you're a quarterback at a Power 5 school, a volleyball star with a huge TikTok following, or a track athlete building a brand on YouTube—NIL has created opportunities that didn't exist even a few years ago. And while that's something to celebrate, it's also something to approach with serious preparation.

Because here's the thing: **this isn't just a rule change—it's a complete game changer**.

When the NCAA finally opened the doors to NIL in July 2021, everything shifted. Athletes suddenly became entrepreneurs. Influencers. Brand ambassadors. Business owners. That means you're now not just managing your time and talent—you're managing income, contracts, taxes, marketing, and your personal brand.

And while everyone loves to talk about the highlights—signing a deal, doing a photo shoot, cashing your first check—**very few people talk about the responsibility that comes with it**.

Let's be clear: NIL is a *business*. And in business, people are expected to read the fine print, file taxes, manage spending, negotiate contracts, and plan for the future. That's what professionals do. And if you're earning NIL money—even if it's just a few hundred dollars—**you're a professional now, too.**

But don't get overwhelmed. This chapter—and this entire book—is here to walk you through it.

We'll explore:

- What NIL actually is and isn't
- The key differences between NIL deals and pro athlete contracts
- Common types of NIL opportunities (and how to evaluate them)
- The responsibilities and risks that come with earning money as a student-athlete
- Why you should think twice before saying "yes" to every offer that hits your DMs

We'll also talk about some of the **unwritten rules** of NIL. Things like:

- How to protect your personal brand
- How to avoid "shiny object syndrome" (not every flashy deal is a smart one)
- Why trying to keep up with teammates or influencers can lead to financial regret
- How to build relationships, not just cash grabs

And finally, we'll dig into one of the most important concepts you can learn: **how NIL can be the launchpad for your future—not just a payday for your present**. Because whether you go pro or not, the way you handle money, branding, and decision-making now will follow you long after your playing days are over.

In short: NIL is not just about the opportunity. It's about the *strategy*.

You've already proven that you can compete. Now it's time to make sure you're competing *smart*—not just hard. Because this is no longer just a game. It's your business. It's your future. And it's your responsibility to learn how to win on and off the field.

NIL = Free Agency Meets Entrepreneurship

Think of NIL like this: **it's part free agency, part entrepreneurship—and all business.**

In pro sports, free agency means you've got leverage. Teams want your talent, and they're willing to pay for it. You get to make choices, negotiate deals, and pick what's best for you. Now, thanks to NIL, *you* have that kind of power—*while you're still in college.*

But there's a twist: you're not just an athlete anymore. You're now the CEO of *You, Inc.* That's where the entrepreneurship comes in.

You are the product. Your name is the brand. Your social media is your marketing. Your performance is your proof of value. And everything from how you carry yourself to how you spend your money affects the value of your business.

Sound overwhelming? It can be. But it can also be one of the most rewarding things you'll ever do—if you approach it with the right mindset.

Let's break it down.

Free Agency Mindset

In a free agency situation, the athlete is in control. They have choices. But to make good choices, you need information. You need to know your worth, understand the market, and be surrounded by a good team of advisors and agents who have your best interests in mind.

With NIL, you're not just taking any deal that hits your DMs. You're evaluating offers, negotiating terms, and making sure it aligns with your values, schedule, and goals. You're also protecting your eligibility and academic standing while juggling classes, training, and a social life.

That's why every deal isn't always a "good" deal. Just because someone's offering you $1,000 to post a video doesn't mean it's worth your time or brand.

In free agency, patience and strategy win the long game. Same here.

Entrepreneurship Reality

Now let's talk about the entrepreneurship side. That NIL money you're earning? It's not a gift. It's *income*. That means you're responsible for:

- Paying taxes (yep—Uncle Sam wants his cut)
- Keeping records
- Tracking business expenses
- Managing cash flow
- Planning for slow seasons

Welcome to being a business owner.

It's not as glamorous as posting a pic with a product, but it's necessary. And the sooner you embrace this mindset, the more confident and prepared you'll be.

Just like entrepreneurs, you'll need to:

- Build your brand
- Network intentionally
- Stay disciplined with spending
- Invest in your future
- Learn to say "no" to protect your "yes"

This is where most athletes mess up. They treat NIL like a quick win instead of a long game. But this isn't Monopoly money—it's your first real exposure to managing income. And how you manage it now will set the tone for the rest of your life

The best athletes understand that **business and sports aren't separate—they're connected.** NIL proves that. If you want to thrive, you need to learn to compete in both.

So yes—NIL = free agency meets entrepreneurship. And *you* are the front office.

Why You're Not Just an Athlete—You're a Business Now

Let's be real. You've always been more than an athlete. You're a student, a leader, a friend, a brand—even if you didn't realize it yet. But now, in the NIL era, it's official: **you are a business**.

This isn't just a metaphor. Legally and financially, you're stepping into a role that requires you to think, act, and operate like a small business owner. And here's what that means: every decision you make—what you post online, the deals you sign, the people you trust with your money—has real-world consequences.

Athletes used to be seen as workers. Now, you're the *product*. You're the marketing team. You're the financial department. You're the brand. The money being offered to you isn't a scholarship bonus or a gift—it's income. And once income enters the picture, so does responsibility.

Would a business sign a deal without reading the contract? Would it spend money without a budget? Would it ignore taxes and hope the IRS doesn't come knocking? Of course not. But unfortunately, that's exactly what many athletes are doing right now. And they're paying the price for it later.

Here's where the game changes.

To run your business well, you need to learn some new plays:

- **Know your value**: What are you bringing to the table—on the field and online?
- **Build your brand**: What do you stand for? How do you want to be known?

- **Manage your money**: How are you spending, saving, investing, and protecting your income?
- **Form your team**: Who's advising you—CPA, agent, financial advisor, attorney?
- **Think long-term**: How can today's NIL money fund your future?

Because here's the truth: if you treat NIL like a hustle, it'll come and go like one. But if you treat it like a business, it can change your life—and maybe even your family's future.

Businesses don't chase quick wins. They think strategically. They build systems. They track performance. And most of all, **they protect the brand**. That means watching what you post. That means turning down bad deals, even if the check looks good. That means being intentional about the image you're projecting—not just for now, but for five years from now.

Some of you reading this may go pro. Some may not. Either way, if you learn to operate like a business now, you'll be light years ahead of your peers—athlete or not. You'll have the discipline, the mindset, and the tools to navigate life with options, not desperation.

You're not just representing a team anymore. You're representing *you*—and every decision matters.

So don't just be the athlete. Be the CEO. Be the brand. Be the business.

Because you already are. Now it's time to start acting like it.

Key Differences Between NIL Income and Pro Contracts

One of the biggest mistakes college athletes make is treating NIL money the same way a pro athlete might treat their rookie contract. Let's be clear: **NIL income and professional contracts are *not* the same thing.**

The moment you start earning money from NIL, you're stepping into a world of financial opportunity—but you're not stepping into the pro leagues (yet). That distinction matters. Here's why.

1. You Don't Have a Team Handling Your Business

When a professional athlete signs a contract, they usually have an entire team behind them: an agent, financial advisor, CPA, attorney, and business manager. Their contracts are negotiated by seasoned professionals. Their taxes are handled. Their finances are often monitored.

With NIL, most student-athletes are figuring it out on their own—or worse, trusting someone unqualified.

You might have an NIL manager, a parent, or a friend helping you, but most college athletes don't have a full financial support system. That means it's on *you* to learn the basics: how to read a contract, track income, and file taxes.

2. NIL Income Is Self-Employment Income

Professional athletes receive a salary (W-2 income) from their teams, which means taxes are automatically withheld. They're employees.

But **NIL money is usually 1099 income**, which means:

- You're considered self-employed
- No one's taking taxes out of your check
- You're responsible for tracking every dollar
- You need to pay *quarterly* estimated taxes (yes, every three months)

If you don't plan ahead, you could owe thousands when tax season hits.

3. No Guaranteed Contracts

In the pros, contracts often come with guarantees. Even if you get injured or cut, certain portions of your income are protected.

NIL deals rarely offer guarantees. Most are short-term, performance-based, and dependent on you meeting specific deliverables—like posting on social media, showing up to events, or wearing branded gear. If you miss a deadline or violate the terms, that money can disappear *real quick*.

4. NIL Has to Fit Around Your Schedule

As a student-athlete, your first responsibility is your sport and your academics. Unlike pro athletes, you don't have an off season that's truly "off." NIL deals must fit into your already packed schedule. Balancing school, practice, training, games, travel, and now business obligations requires time management, discipline, and prioritization.

5. You Still Have to Protect Your Eligibility

Pro athletes don't have to worry about NCAA compliance, university guidelines, or scholarship eligibility. **You do.**

Accepting the wrong deal could jeopardize your eligibility. There are rules about what you can promote, who you can partner with, and how deals are structured. That's why reading the fine print—and getting professional guidance—is so important.

Final Word

NIL is a great opportunity, but it's not a pro contract. It's an introduction to the business of being an athlete. If you treat it seriously now, you'll be more prepared when those pro opportunities *do* come—or better yet, you'll be set for life no matter what.

Learn the differences, play smart, and protect your future.

Questions to Ask Your Coach and University About NIL

When it comes to NIL, one of the biggest mistakes student-athletes make is assuming someone else is going to guide them through it. The truth is, **no one is going to care about your financial success more than you do**. That's why it's on you to ask questions—and the *right* ones.

Just like you'd study film before a big game, you need to study your resources, your rights, and your responsibilities when it comes to NIL. That starts with knowing what your university offers—and what it doesn't.

Here are some key questions you need to ask your **coaching staff, athletic department, compliance officer, or university NIL coordinator**:

1. "Do we have NIL education or workshops available for athletes?"

Some schools have built full NIL support programs—others are still figuring it out. Ask if your school offers:

- Financial literacy courses
- Contract negotiation education
- Guest speakers or professional advisors
- Resources on branding, taxes, and marketing

If the answer is no, that's okay—but now you know it's up to you to get educated. (Good thing you're reading this book.)

2. "Who pays for disability insurance if I get hurt?"

This is a BIG one.

If you get injured, do you know what happens to your NIL deals? Do you know how your future earnings could be affected? Some schools offer **disability insurance** to protect athletes with pro potential. Others don't.

Ask directly:

- "Do we have disability insurance options for athletes?"
- "If not, can you help me explore coverage on my own?"
- "Can NIL income be used to buy private insurance?"

Disability coverage is protection for **the future you**—especially if your body is your business.

3. "Do you provide any help or resources for filing taxes?"

You already know that NIL income is taxable. But are you expected to figure it out alone?

Ask:

- "Does the university help with tax prep or connect us with a CPA?"
- "Do you offer any guidance for quarterly tax payments?"
- "Are there workshops on what to track and save for tax season?"

Even just being pointed to a trusted accountant could save you from a huge tax headache.

4. "Are there trusted professionals I can talk to about investing, budgeting, and saving?"

You shouldn't have to rely on TikTok or social media for financial advice. Ask your program if they have vetted financial professionals who:

- Understand student-athletes
- Operate as fiduciaries (that means they're legally required to act in your best interest)
- Can explain budgeting and investing in a way that makes sense

You're building a business around your name. That business needs guidance, strategy, and protection.

Bottom Line: Be Proactive

Your coach may not have all the answers—but asking these questions lets your program know you're serious. You're not just here to play. You're here to build a foundation for life.

This is your career. Ask the questions that protect it.

Financial Fundamentals – Your Preseason Camp

Every athlete knows that championships aren't won during the season—they're won in the off season. It's the early mornings, the extra reps, the uncomfortable workouts, and the discipline behind the scenes that lead to those big moments under the lights. That's what *preseason camp* is all about. It's where you build the habits that carry you through game time.

Financial literacy works the same way.

Before you start thinking about NIL deals, taxes, investing, or contracts, you need to master the basics. This section is your preseason. It's where we get your financial muscles warm, your mindset locked in, and your playbook in place. Because no matter how big the opportunity is, if your foundation isn't solid, the whole thing can fall apart.

In the coming chapters, we'll walk through the *core skills* that every student-athlete needs—not just to survive NIL, but to thrive long after your college career is over.

We'll start with **budgeting**—aka your financial game plan. Just like you wouldn't step on the field without knowing your assignment, you can't spend money without a clear understanding of your income and expenses. A budget isn't something that limits you—it *frees you*. It tells your money where to go so you don't wonder where it went.

Next, we'll tackle **credit** and **emergency funds**. Think of your credit score like your coach's trust level—hard to earn, easy to lose, and incredibly important for your future. Whether it's renting an apartment, buying a car, or applying for a loan later in life, your credit reputation will follow you. And emergency funds? That's your backup quarterback. You may not need it every game, but when life throws a curve ball, you'll be glad you have one.

We'll also show you how to **pull your credit report**, open your **first checking and savings account**, and develop the habits that help you stay ready—not just financially, but mentally.

This section is about preparation, discipline, and awareness. It's about building the confidence to say, *"I know how to handle my money."* Because once that confidence sets in, the rest becomes easier. Every NIL decision, every tax filing, every investment opportunity becomes something you approach with clarity instead of confusion.

You've already shown that you're willing to work hard for your athletic success. Now it's time to bring that same energy to your financial life. The earlier you start building good habits, the longer your money will work for you—and the less likely you are to fall into the traps that have sidelined too many athletes before you.

So grab your notebook, clear your distractions, and lock in. This is your preseason financial camp.

Let's get these fundamentals right—because game day is coming.

Introduction: Why This Book Matters

When I was a student-athlete, no one pulled me aside to talk about credit scores, taxes, budgeting, or investing. We talked about game plans, workouts, and winning. But not once did someone show me how to manage a scholarship refund, negotiate a deal, or prepare for life after sports. And back then, NIL didn't even exist.

Now, everything has changed.

Today's student-athletes are being offered life-changing opportunities—sponsorships, social media deals, merchandise, and endorsements—while still in college. But for every athlete cashing in on their Name, Image, and Likeness, there are dozens more unsure of how to handle it. I've seen too many athletes lose their momentum because they never learned the rules of the financial game.

That's why I wrote this book.

Financial Literacy For NIL is your playbook for mastering money while navigating the fast-paced world of NIL. Whether you're signing your first endorsement deal or just trying to understand how taxes work, this book was written for **you**. It's not just about getting the bag—it's about keeping it, growing it, and making it last long after the final whistle.

We'll cover everything from budgeting and credit to investing, insurance, taxes, and long-term wealth-building. We'll talk about how to protect yourself legally, how to spot bad contracts, and how to say "no" to financial pressure from friends and family. You'll also learn the importance of having the right team around you—agents, CPAs, advisors—and the questions you need to ask before trusting anyone with your money.

I'll also be honest with you: NIL won't last forever. You might go pro. You might not. But what you do with your NIL money today can set you up for freedom and financial peace tomorrow. Even if you only earn a few thousand dollars from NIL, you can turn that into something meaningful if you make smart decisions now.

As a former Division I athlete, financial advisor, and advocate for student-athletes, I created this book to bridge the gap between talent and financial knowledge. I've made mistakes. I've learned lessons. I've helped others avoid pitfalls and build lasting success.

Now it's your turn.

This is more than a book. It's a wake-up call, a blueprint, and a resource. Let's make sure you're not just winning on the field—but off of it too.

Welcome to *Financial Literacy For NIL.*

You've trained your whole life to succeed on the field. Now it's time to train for the game of life.

You've lifted weights in the off season, studied film, memorized playbooks, recovered from injury, and competed under pressure. You've done what few others could do: stay disciplined enough to earn a scholarship or roster spot at the college level. That's not luck—that's work. That's intentional preparation.

But here's the thing nobody tells you: the habits that made you successful in your sport are the same habits you'll need to succeed in life. Focus. Consistency. Sacrifice. And yes—training.

Financial success doesn't just show up. It's not about luck or talent. It's about developing the right habits, understanding the rules, and making smart, consistent decisions over time. The same way you've studied your opponent's defense, you now have to learn to study your spending. Just like you analyze your strengths and weaknesses on the field, you'll need to assess your financial situation off the field.

This book is here to coach you through it.

We're going to treat money like a game—because it is one. And if you don't know the rules, someone else will win while you're still trying to figure out how to play. NIL has changed the landscape, but what hasn't changed is the need for discipline. Without financial literacy, NIL can hurt you more than it helps.

Think of this book as your off season program. You won't master everything overnight, but if you show up consistently, the results will come. By the end of this journey, you'll know how to budget, understand your taxes, evaluate NIL deals, build credit, invest early, and protect your future with insurance and smart decision-making. You'll know what questions to ask your agent, CPA, or financial advisor—and you'll be equipped to spot a bad deal from a mile away.

And let's be clear: this isn't just about stacking money during college. This is about playing the long game. Most athletes won't go pro—and even those who do won't stay there forever. Careers end. Contracts expire. Your body has a limit. But your money doesn't—if you learn how to make it work for you.

If you can grasp these concepts now, you won't just win financially—you'll have options. Options to say no to bad opportunities. Options to support your family. Options to invest in yourself, your education, your dreams, your community. This is about freedom.

The goal of this book isn't perfection—it's preparation. I want to help you avoid the financial mistakes so many athletes have made. I want you to be able to look back ten, twenty, even thirty years from now and thank your younger self for taking this seriously.

So as we step into Chapter 1, remember this: you've already proven that you're willing to work hard. You already know how to compete. Now, let's channel that same energy into building the kind of financial future you—and your family—deserve.

Chapter 1: Budgeting Your Financial Playbook

If your money had a coach, it would be your budget.

Just like you'd never go into a game without a playbook, you shouldn't go through life without a financial one. A budget is your strategy for how to spend, save, and grow your money. It's not about restriction—it's about control. It gives your money purpose, direction, and discipline—just like your sport gives structure to your training.

Why You Need a Budget (Even If You Think You Don't)

You might be thinking, "I'm not making that much yet, do I really need a budget?"

Yes. Especially now.

NIL money can come in fast—but it can disappear even faster. A budget helps you:

- Track where your money is going
- Make intentional decisions instead of emotional ones
- Prepare for taxes, emergencies, and future goals
- Avoid being the athlete who's broke six months after the season ends

Remember: budgeting now puts *future you* in a position to win.

The Budget Breakdown: Your Starting Lineup

Here's a simple way to think of your money using sports roles:

- Income = Your offense. This is the money coming in from NIL deals, campus jobs, scholarships, or family support.
- Fixed expenses = Your starters. These are bills you have to pay every month like rent, phone, groceries, insurance, subscriptions.
- Variable expenses = Your bench players. These include entertainment, clothes, dining out, or gifts—things that change month to month.

Savings = Your MVP. Every dollar you save now is a future assist to your older self. Even if you just save $50/month, it adds up.

The 50/30/20 Rule (Game Plan Format)

This is a basic rule you can adjust to fit your life:

- 50% of income → needs (rent, food, transportation)
- 30% → wants (fun money, gear, going out)
- 20% → savings & goals (emergency fund, taxes, investments)

If NIL income is unpredictable, use the "pay yourself first" method—automatically save a set amount from each check before you spend anything.

Tools That Help

You don't have to do it all manually. Try these apps:

- Mint – Free budgeting app that links to your accounts
- Rocket Money – Helps cancel subscriptions you don't use
- Zogo – Gamified financial learning
- Google Sheets or Excel – Simple and customizable

Final Whistle: Game-Winning Tips

- Know your numbers. Check your spending weekly. Treat it like film study.
- Set goals. Want to save for a car? Invest? Start a brand? Budget for it.
- Be honest. Track *everything*. That $6 coffee habit adds up faster than you think.
- Adjust monthly. Your budget should evolve as your income changes. NIL checks aren't always consistent—be ready.

You wouldn't let your team go into a game without a plan—so don't let your money step on the field without one either.

Budgeting is the first step toward financial freedom. Now that your playbook is built, let's get to work on executing it.

Budgeting Is Like a Game Plan — You Don't Just Run Plays Randomly

Imagine showing up to a big game without a game plan.

No script. No strategy. No idea who's starting or what plays you're running. You just take the field and hope it all works out. Sounds ridiculous, right?

Well, that's exactly what it's like to go through life without a budget.

A budget is your financial game plan. It gives you structure, direction, and the ability to make smart decisions under pressure. Without it, you're just reacting—and in sports, reacting without preparation usually leads to losses.

You wouldn't show up to a game and run plays just because they sound good in the moment. You run what's been practiced, prepared, and tailored to the situation. Budgeting works the same way. It helps you allocate your money with intention—not just vibes.

Let's take it a step further.

The Offensive Coordinator = You

You are the offensive coordinator of your financial life. Every paycheck is a new possession. The question is—what are you doing with it?

Just like in football or basketball, you only get a certain number of possessions (or dollars). Some are big plays (like an NIL deal), others are small gains (maybe a campus job or scholarship refund). But you still need a plan for each one.

If you blow your money on impulse spending—new shoes, random fast food, upgrades you didn't plan for—you're running trick plays on 1st-and-10 every time. It might work once in a while, but over time, you're losing yardage.

With a budget, you call the plays that move you down the field:

- Paying rent = picking up a first down
- Saving for taxes = running the ball to control the clock
- Investing early = hitting a deep shot for long-term gains
- Emergency fund = your audible when the defense throws a blitz

Breakdowns Happen When There's No Plan

Without a game plan, what happens? Confusion. Missed assignments. Turnovers. That's how you end up over drafting your account, forgetting to save for taxes, or realizing you have $40 left to survive the next two weeks.

Your budget keeps you grounded. It helps you read the defense—aka life's unexpected expenses—and adjust before it's too late.

Your Budget Should Be Like a Weekly Practice Schedule

Just like you don't prepare for the season one time and call it good, you shouldn't create a budget once and forget it. You have to review it, tweak it, and stay consistent. Look at your spending like you'd review film. What worked last month? Where did you blow coverage (aka overspend)? How can you tighten things up?

It doesn't have to be fancy. It just has to be real. You're the coach, the player, and the GM of your life—and a solid budget is how you run a championship organization.

So the next time you get paid, don't just wing it.

Call your plays with purpose. Budget with confidence. And run your financial offense like a pro.

That's how you win—on and off the field.

Know Your "Offense" (Income) and "Defense" (Expenses)

In any sport, you can't win without understanding both sides of the game.

Sure, a high-powered offense might put points on the board—but if your defense can't stop anything, you're still losing. The same goes for your finances. It's not just about how much money you make (offense)—it's about how much you keep and where it goes (defense).

Let's break it down.

Your Offense = Your Income

Your offense is your income—the money coming in. Just like in a game, you need to know your play makers and your scoring ability. For student-athletes, your offense might include:

- NIL deals
- Sponsorships or brand partnerships
- Campus jobs or side hustles
- Scholarship refund checks (if any)
- Financial support from family
- Social media monetization or merch sales

Even if your income isn't consistent—maybe you get one big NIL payment every few months—it's still your job to know what's coming in, when it's coming, and how much you can realistically rely on. You wouldn't call plays without knowing who's available on your roster. The same applies here.

Tip: Write down every income source, estimate what you earn monthly, and build your game plan from there. That's your offensive scouting report.

Your Defense = Your Expenses

Your defense is your spending—the money going out. And just like a weak defense will cost your team wins, reckless spending will blow up your financial game plan.

Expenses come in two types:

- Fixed expenses: These are your everyday starters—rent, utilities, groceries, phone bill, subscriptions. They're predictable and show up every month.
- Variable expenses: These are your wildcard players—eating out, shopping, travel, entertainment. They change month to month and are usually where things get out of control if you're not careful.

Every dollar that goes out is a "point" against your budget. If your defense isn't tight, your offense doesn't stand a chance—no matter how much you're making.

That's why tracking expenses is just as important as tracking income.

Winning Happens When You Control Both Sides

Let's say you sign an NIL deal and get $5,000. That's a strong offensive play. But if you turn around and spend $4,000 on new clothes, a weekend trip, and a lease on a car you can't really afford, then your defense just gave up a huge touchdown.

What does that lead to? Financial losses. Overdraft fees. Missed payments. Tax issues. Stress. Regret.

But if you put together a budget that balances both your income and your expenses—just like a great team game plan—you'll start stacking wins: savings, peace of mind, options, and freedom.

Final Thought: Balance Wins Championships

The best teams aren't just great at scoring—they know how to protect the lead.

Know your offense. Lock in your defense. And treat your money like a team that's playing for a title—because your future is the trophy.

Fixed Costs = Your Starting Lineup (Rent, Phone, Food)

Every team has a starting lineup—the players you can count on to show up every game, handle the fundamentals, and play a consistent role. They might not always be flashy, but they're dependable. You build your strategy around them because they're always on the court, field, or track.

In your financial life, your fixed costs are the same. These are the non-negotiables—the bills that show up every month, whether you're balling or broke.

They include things like:

- Rent or housing
- Utilities (electricity, water, Wi-Fi)
- Phone bill
- Groceries or meal plan
- Insurance (if you pay your own health, car, or renter's insurance)
- Subscriptions (Netflix, Spotify, Hulu—anything that's billed regularly)

You don't get to *not* pay these. And if you do miss a payment? Just like benching your point guard last-minute—it throws off your whole system.

Why Fixed Costs Matter

Your fixed costs are what you need to survive and stay stable. When you build your budget, these are the first things you account for. Just like a coach builds a game plan around the strengths of their starters, you build your financial plan around what it takes to cover your fixed expenses.

If you don't know these numbers off the top of your head, it's time to find out.

Sit down and list every recurring monthly payment. Total it up. This is your financial baseline.

It's the minimum you need to make just to keep the lights on—literally.

Why You Can't Afford to Ignore Them

Imagine not knowing who your starters are before a big game. You get out there and realize you're short a receiver or missing your power forward. That's what it's like to go through the month without knowing your fixed expenses—you're guessing, hoping, and usually scrambling at the end.

That's when overdrafts happen. That's when rent's late. That's when you say, "Wait, where did my money go?"

But when you *do* know your starting lineup, you play with confidence. You know what you can afford and what you can't. You know how much is left for fun, savings, or investing once the essentials are handled.

Pro Tip: Keep Your Starters Affordable

If your starting lineup is too expensive, your bench (the fun stuff) suffers—and so does your overall game. If you're spending $1,200/month on rent and you're only earning $1,500/month from NIL, you've already lost the game in the first quarter.

Choose affordable housing. Keep your phone plan simple. Don't overload your monthly budget with unnecessary subscriptions. Start with the essentials, then build from there.

Final Word: Know Who You Can Count On

Your starters win the game by showing up and doing their job. In your finances, your fixed costs show up every month. Whether you're having a good money month or not, they'll be there.

So build your budget around them. Respect them. And make sure they don't take up so much space that there's nothing left for the rest of your team.

Know your starting lineup—and pay them first.

Variable Costs = Your Bench Players (Clothes, Going Out, Streaming Services)

Every team has bench players—the ones who don't start every game, but still play an important role. They come off the bench, bring energy, and can make a big impact... when managed properly. But if your bench takes over the game and doesn't follow the plan, things get out of control fast.

That's exactly what variable costs are in your financial life.

These are the expenses that don't happen on a fixed schedule. They change from week to week or month to month based on your choices, mood, or moment. They include things like:

- Eating out
- Clothing and shoes
- Streaming services and apps
- Concerts, clubs, or trips
- Snacks, coffee runs, or spontaneous Amazon orders

In short, they're the "fun stuff." They're also the most dangerous part of your budget if you don't keep them in check.

Why Variable Costs Matter

Just like a good bench can be the difference-maker in a close game, your variable spending can make or break your monthly financial performance. There's nothing wrong with going out with friends, buying new gear, or enjoying a weekend getaway—as long as it's part of your game plan.

The problem happens when your bench tries to take over the starting lineup.

If you're spending more on takeout, parties, and gear than you are on rent, groceries, and bills, you're running a broken system—and that's when your financial game starts falling apart.

Track Your Bench Minutes (and Money)

In sports, coaches track how many minutes each player gets. You should do the same with your variable costs.

Look back over the last month and ask:

- How many times did I eat out?
- How much did I spend on clothes or shoes?
- How many subscriptions do I actually use?
- Did any of these purchases really move me closer to my goals?

The answer might surprise you.

You'll probably find out that a lot of your "money leaks" come from your bench—not your starters. It's the $10 here, $15 there that adds up to hundreds by the end of the month.

Set Limits, Not Elimination

Just like a coach doesn't bench all their players forever, you don't need to eliminate all your fun spending. The key is knowing your limit.

Give yourself a monthly or weekly "bench budget"—a set amount you allow yourself to enjoy without guilt. Once that number's up, you pause until next payday.

It's not about punishment. It's about control. You're still enjoying life—but now you're doing it without sabotaging your future.

Final Word: Keep Your Bench in Check

Your bench players are valuable—but they shouldn't run the team.

Your variable expenses add flavor to life—but they need structure, too. Use them wisely. Rotate them in when appropriate. Just don't let them take over the game plan.

Because when your starters and your bench work together with discipline and purpose?

That's how championship budgets are built.

Tools: Use Mint, Rocket Money, or a Simple Spreadsheet to Track Your Budget

Great athletes watch film.

They study their performance, analyze the tape, and make adjustments. Why? Because you can't fix what you don't track. It's the same with your money.

If you're not tracking your spending, you're just guessing. And in both sports and life, guessing rarely wins games.

Luckily, in today's world, you don't need to be a financial expert or math wizard to track your money. There are tools—some free, some paid—that make budgeting simple, visual, and easy to stay on top of. Here are a few that can help you build the financial version of your highlight reel.

1. Mint – Your Personal Finance Assistant

Think of Mint like your team's analytics coach. It automatically tracks your spending by linking to your bank account, credit card, and other financial tools. It organizes your purchases into categories—like food, transportation, and entertainment—so you can see exactly where your money is going.

What Mint helps you do:

- Set monthly spending limits
- Get alerts when you're approaching your budget
- Monitor your credit score for free
- Track upcoming bills and due dates

Why athletes love it: It's hands-off. Once you link your accounts, Mint does the tracking for you, so you can focus on your game and still know your money situation at a glance.

2. Rocket Money – Cancel Subscriptions and Cut Waste

If Mint is your analytics coach, Rocket Money is your team's cap space manager. It looks for subscriptions or recurring charges that you might not even realize are draining your account and gives you the option to cancel them with one tap.

What Rocket Money helps you do:

- See every subscription you're paying for
- Cancel services you don't use directly through the app
- Set spending goals and receive progress updates
- Get insight into your spending habits

Why athletes love it: It finds money leaks you didn't even know you had—like that free trial you forgot to cancel, or that streaming service you don't really use anymore.

3. Google Sheets or Excel – The Old School Game Plan

If you like things simple, a basic spreadsheet might be your go-to.
You can set up a table with:

- Monthly income (NIL deals, side jobs, family help)
- Fixed costs (rent, phone, groceries)
- Variable costs (going out, travel, clothes)
- Savings goals (taxes, emergency fund, investments)

This method requires more manual entry—but it forces you to *pay attention,* which helps build discipline. Think of it like watching film on yourself every week—it may be time-consuming, but it's also incredibly valuable.

Final Word: The Best Tool Is the One You'll Actually Use

You don't need every app. You don't need to build the perfect spreadsheet.
You just need something you'll check regularly—just like your practice schedule or game plan.

Because the better you track your spending, the better decisions you'll make. And the better decisions you make, the closer you get to winning the financial game.

Pick your tool. Learn it. Use it. Own your budget like you own your sport.

Lesson: If You Fail to Plan Your Money, Your Money Will Run Its Own Plays—Bad Ones

Every team has a game plan going into a big matchup. Coaches break down film, study tendencies, create strategies, and script plays. The more detailed the plan, the more confident the players. But what happens if you walk into the game with no plan at all?

Chaos.

Blown assignments. Missed routes. Poor execution. You get outplayed and out coached. The same thing happens when you don't plan your money—your money starts running its own plays, and trust me, they're not winning plays.

If you don't tell your money where to go, it'll disappear before you know it.

Let Me Tell You a Quick Story...

I once worked with a student-athlete who signed his first NIL deal—a $10,000 payment for a social media campaign. He was hyped. Rightfully so. That kind of money is life-changing when you're in college.

But here's the problem: he didn't have a financial game plan. No budget. No savings strategy. No tax prep. No boundaries.

Within two months, it was gone.

He bought new clothes, upgraded his phone, flew his friends out for a weekend trip, started DoorDashing every meal, and didn't track a single expense. By the time tax season rolled around, he owed thousands—and had nothing saved to cover it.

He didn't run the plays. The money ran him.

What "Bad Money Plays" Look Like

If you don't plan your money, here's what typically happens:

- You overspend on stuff that doesn't even matter in a week.
- You forget about upcoming bills and end up scrambling to pay rent or phone bills.
- You don't save for taxes, so you're blindsided in April.
- You never build an emergency fund, so when your car breaks down or you get injured, you're broke and stressed.
- You miss out on investing early, which means your money doesn't grow.

It's like giving your opponent the ball over and over again with no defense on the field.

How to Run Winning Plays with Your Money

Winning with money isn't about being perfect. It's about being prepared. That means:

- Creating a simple budget (your playbook)
- Tracking income and expenses weekly (your film study)
- Setting savings goals (your season targets)
- Reviewing and adjusting monthly (your halftime adjustments)

You don't have to get everything right the first time. You just need to take control.

Final Word: Be the Quarterback, Not the Spectator

Money can either be your teammate or your opponent—it all depends on how you treat it.

If you plan your money, it'll move with purpose. It'll block for you, protect you, and set you up to score. But if you don't? It'll fumble the bag, throw pick-sixes, and leave you wondering where it all went.

So run the play. Lead the huddle. Take control.

Because when it comes to your financial future, you're the quarterback now.

Chapter 2: Credit & Emergency Funds Your Backup Plan

In sports, it's not just your starters that matter—it's your depth. Your backups, your second unit, your insurance policy when someone gets injured or something unexpected happens. Every successful team has a plan B.

In your financial life, credit and emergency savings are your backup plan. You may not think about them every day, but when something breaks down or you get hit with unexpected expenses, they're the difference between staying in the game and getting benched by life.

Let's break down why both are critical.

Credit: Your Financial Reputation

Credit is like your coach's trust in you. It takes time to build, but one bad decision can destroy it fast. Your credit score tells lenders (and eventually landlords, car dealers, and even some employers) how responsible you are with money.

A good credit score helps you:

- Rent an apartment
- Buy a car
- Qualify for lower interest rates
- Get approved for a business loan or mortgage later in life

Your credit score is made up of:

- Payment history (35%) – Do you pay bills on time?
- Credit utilization (30%) – Are you using too much of your credit limit?
- Length of credit history (15%) – How long have your accounts been open?
- Credit mix (10%) – Do you have different types of accounts (credit cards, loans)?
- New credit inquiries (10%) – How often are you applying for credit?

Start Simple:

- Open a student-friendly credit card with a low limit ($300–$500)
- Use it only for small purchases (like gas or groceries)
- Pay it off in full every month—not just the minimum

Think of it like lifting weights. Done right, it builds strength. But if you don't handle it properly? You'll pull something and set yourself back.

Emergency Funds: Your Financial Backup QB

Now let's talk about the emergency fund—your financial bench player.

An emergency fund is money you set aside for the unexpected:

- Flat tires
- Medical bills
- Travel home for a family emergency
- A late NIL payment
- Losing your phone or breaking your laptop

The goal: Save $500 to $1,000 to start. Eventually, aim for 2–3 months of essential expenses.

This isn't money you touch for concert tickets or a new pair of kicks. It's for emergencies only. You can keep it in a separate savings account to avoid the temptation of dipping into it.

Why These Two Matter Together

If something goes wrong—and it *will* at some point—credit and emergency funds keep you from falling apart. If you don't have emergency savings, you'll probably rely on your credit card. If your credit is bad, you won't even have that option.

But when both are in place? You have peace of mind, confidence, and the freedom to focus on your sport, school, and NIL opportunities without constantly worrying about money.

Final Word: Stay Ready So You Don't Have to Get Ready

Your starting lineup may be strong, but your backups keep the season alive. Build credit. Stack savings. Protect your future.

Because when life sends a blitz, your backup plan is what keeps you in the game.

Analogy: Your Credit Score Is Like Your Coach's Trust—Hard to Earn, Easy to Lose

If you've ever played for a tough coach, you know this already: trust is everything.

You don't just walk into the gym or onto the field and become the go-to player. You earn it—through effort, discipline, and consistency. You show up early, do the little things right, learn the system, and prove you can be counted on. And once you've earned your coach's trust, you're given more responsibility. More minutes. More opportunities.

But mess it up? Show up late. Miss practice. Skip a workout. Blow off a team meeting—and you can lose that trust overnight. And getting it back? That's a long, uphill climb.

Your credit score works the same way.

What Is a Credit Score, Really?

A credit score is a number that tells lenders—like banks, landlords, car dealerships, and future business partners—how much they can trust you with money.

It's built based on your history of:

- Paying bills on time
- Managing credit responsibly
- Keeping your debt low
- Avoiding risky financial behavior

Your credit score ranges from 300 to 850. The higher it is, the more financially trustworthy you're considered. Just like a coach trusts you to take the game-winning shot or lead the team, lenders trust you to borrow money—and pay it back.

Why It Matters (Even Now)

You might be thinking, "I'm in college. Why should I care about credit right now?"

Here's why:

- Want to rent an apartment off-campus? They'll check your credit.
- Want to finance a car later on? They'll check your credit.
- Want to open a business or get a mortgage one day? You guessed it—credit.
- Some employers even check credit during the hiring process.

Credit is your reputation. It doesn't just affect your finances—it affects your options.

Building Trust: The Right Way to Start

Just like a coach doesn't throw you into a championship game without seeing how you perform in practice, lenders won't trust you with big loans until you prove yourself with small ones.

Start small:

- Open a student credit card with a low limit.
- Use it for gas, groceries, or one small recurring bill.
- Pay it off in full every single month.
- Don't max it out—keep your usage below 30% of your limit.

Over time, you build a record of responsibility. Your score rises. You get more opportunities. You become the trusted starter.

Losing Trust: The Fastest Way to Fall

Miss a payment? Max out your card? Open too many accounts too quickly? That score will drop *fast*—and the damage can last for years.

Just like a coach remembers who fumbled in the fourth quarter, the credit system remembers your mistakes. But unlike your coach, the credit system won't give you another shot unless you put in serious time and effort to rebuild.

Final Word: Earn It, Keep It, Protect It

Your credit score is your financial trust score. And just like with your coach, it takes time to earn, a moment to lose, and a long road to rebuild.

So start today. Be disciplined. Show up. Handle your money like a pro—and your credit score will show the world that you're ready for the big leagues.

Learn to Pull Your Credit Report at AnnualCreditReport.com

Let's keep it real: you can't fix what you don't see.

Your credit report is like your personal scouting report. It shows your financial history—every credit card, every payment (on time or late), every loan, and every hard inquiry made when someone checked your credit. It's what lenders, landlords, and even some employers use to decide if they can trust you with money, a lease, or even a job.

That's why it's crucial that you check it regularly—and check it yourself.

Think of it like watching film on your own game. You're not just looking for highlights—you're checking for weaknesses, blind spots, and things that need cleaning up. That's how you improve.

Here's How You Do It:

Go to AnnualCreditReport.com

This is the only official website authorized by federal law to provide your free credit reports from the three major credit bureaus:

- Equifax
- Experian
- TransUnion

You're entitled to one free credit report per bureau every 12 months, and during certain periods (like COVID), they may offer free reports more frequently.

Here's a step-by-step walkthrough:

1. Visit the site: www.annualcreditreport.com
2. Click "Request your free credit reports"
3. Fill out your information: name, address, Social Security number, and date of birth (this is secure and necessary to verify your identity).
4. Select which reports you want to view (you can choose all three, or

spread them out through the year).

5. Answer identity verification questions based on your credit history (they might ask about old addresses or loans).

Boom—you now have access to your full credit report.

What You're Looking For

Once you're in, you want to check for:

- Accounts in your name: Are they accurate? Do they belong to you?
- Payment history: Any missed or late payments? Mistakes?
- Inquiries: Who's pulled your credit recently?
- Collections: Any unpaid debts you didn't know about?

If something doesn't look right, dispute it immediately. There are clear instructions on the site to report errors—and fixing even one mistake could boost your credit score fast.

Why This Matters Now

Even if you've never used a credit card, you could have a credit report. Student loans, car loans, or someone co-signing for you could have already started building your credit history. And in some unfortunate cases, identity theft can start your credit journey for you—without your knowledge.

Knowing what's on your report keeps you in control. It's how you protect your financial reputation before it ever gets damaged.

Final Word: Check It Like You Check Your Stats

You wouldn't go a whole season without checking your stats or watching film. Don't go through college without checking your credit.

Pull your report. Learn what it means. Fix what's broken. Build what's missing.

This is how you scout yourself financially—and it's one of the most powerful habits you can build for the rest of your life.

Build a $1,000 Emergency Fund — It's Your Backup QB When Life Blitzes You

In football, every great team knows the value of a solid backup quarterback. You hope you never have to use them, but when your starter gets injured or the defense throws an unexpected blitz, that backup steps in and keeps the team from falling apart.

In life, your emergency fund is your backup quarterback. It's not flashy. It doesn't get much attention. But when the unexpected happens—and trust me, it will—you'll be glad you had it ready.

Let's talk about what it is, why it matters, and how to build it.

What Is an Emergency Fund?

An emergency fund is a small stash of cash set aside for one purpose only: to cover unexpected expenses that could throw your whole game off.

We're talking about things like:

- A flat tire or car repair
- Emergency travel home
- A broken phone or lost laptop
- A late NIL payment or delayed refund check
- A medical bill you didn't see coming

These moments don't announce themselves. They show up like a surprise blitz—fast and disruptive. If you don't have a financial backup in place, you're scrambling. That's when people start swiping credit cards they can't pay off, asking others for money, or falling behind on bills.

Why $1,000?

We recommend building a $1,000 emergency fund to start because it's:

- Achievable – You don't need to be rich to save it.
- Strategic – It's enough to cover *most* emergencies without wiping you out.
- Stabilizing – It gives you confidence and breathing room.

It's like having your backup QB warmed up and ready on the sideline. You might never need them—but if you do, they're ready to go.

Where to Keep It

Open a separate savings account (not your main checking account). This makes it harder to spend and easier to protect.

Some options:

- A basic savings account at your current bank
- A high-yield online savings account (pays more interest)
- A credit union or campus-affiliated bank

Do not keep it in cash in a shoebox. Life's not a rap video. You want it safe and accessible, but not tempting.

How to Build It Fast

If $1,000 feels like a lot, don't stress. Start small. Here are a few ways to get there:

- Save $50/week for 5 months
- Take a portion (10–20%) of each NIL or work check and set it aside
- Sell unused clothes, gear, or tech online

- Cut out two impulse buys per week and put that money in savings

Before you know it, your emergency fund is sitting on the bench, ready to play.

Final Word: Don't Wait Until You Need It

You don't wait to train your backup quarterback until your starter is out. You prepare ahead of time.

An emergency fund is the same. It gives you peace of mind, protects your budget, and lets you stay focused on your sport, school, and life—even when the unexpected hits.

So start building yours now. Because when life brings the blitz, you'll want to know your financial backup is ready to take the snap.

Avoid Credit Card Fumbles — Good Debt Can Help You, Bad Debt Will Bench You

In football, nothing kills a drive faster than a fumble. You can be marching down the field, calling all the right plays, and gaining yards—then *boom*—the ball slips out and the momentum is gone. That's exactly what happens when you misuse credit cards. One or two bad moves, and suddenly your financial game plan is out the window.

Let's be clear: credit cards aren't evil. In fact, when used the right way, they can actually help you build your credit score, manage emergencies, and even earn rewards. But if you're not careful? They'll cost you big—and keep you on the financial bench for years.

Good Debt vs. Bad Debt: What's the Difference?

In the world of money, not all debt is created equal. Some debt can help you move forward in life. Other debt will drag you down.

- Good debt is strategic. It includes things like:
- A credit card you pay off in full each month to build credit
- A low-interest student loan with a clear repayment plan
- A business loan that helps you grow your brand or NIL platform
- Bad debt is emotional. It includes:
- High-interest credit cards you carry a balance on
- Buying things you don't need to impress people you don't know
- Maxing out your card without a plan to pay it off

Think of it this way: good debt is like lifting weights with a spotter. It builds your strength if you do it right. Bad debt is like going heavy without a spot—you might look strong at first, but eventually, you'll get pinned.

How to Use Credit Cards Without Fumbling the Bag

1. Start with a low-limit student credit card
2. Look for one with no annual fee and a limit of $300–$500.
3. Only use it for small, essential purchases
4. Think gas, groceries, or one monthly subscription. Not plane tickets to Miami or the newest Jordans.
5. Pay your balance in full every month
6. Not just the minimum. Full payment = no interest charges and maximum credit score growth.
7. Keep your utilization low
8. Try to use less than 30% of your credit limit. If your limit is $500, don't spend more than $150 at a time.
9. Set up automatic payments
10. So you never miss a due date. One missed payment can drop your score 50–100 points.

Why It Matters

Your credit card usage tells future lenders (and even employers and landlords) how financially responsible you are. If you fumble here, it could cost you:

- A car loan
- An apartment
- A lower interest rate
- Your peace of mind

But if you handle it well? You're building the kind of financial trust that opens doors.

Final Word: Protect the Ball

Your credit card is a tool—not a toy. Used wisely, it can move you forward. Used recklessly, it'll have you sitting on the sidelines, trying to recover.

So grip it tight, call the right plays, and avoid the fumble. Because bad debt doesn't just hurt—it benches your financial future.

Part 2: NIL – Managing the Spotlight

Welcome to the big stage.

You've earned the spotlight through your talent, hustle, and discipline—and now, because of NIL (Name, Image, and Likeness), that spotlight comes with opportunity. But here's the truth: opportunity always brings responsibility. And if you're not careful, the same spotlight that helps you shine can also expose you if you're unprepared.

This part of the book is where things get real. We're diving into the business side of being a student-athlete in the NIL era. Whether you're already signing deals or just starting to explore what NIL means, this section will help you protect your brand, make smart money moves, and avoid the common traps that leave so many athletes stuck—or worse, broke.

NIL = Business

Let's be clear: if you're earning money from your name, image, or likeness—you're not just a student-athlete anymore.

You're a brand. You're a business. You're your own agent, manager, and CEO.

But don't let that scare you. You don't need to know everything right away. You just need to treat your NIL opportunities like what they are: real-world business transactions that can either set you up for success or become expensive mistakes.

That's what this section is all about.

Managing the Spotlight

Think of NIL as your introduction to the business world, but with the unique twist of being in the public eye. People are watching—brands, fans, media, and future employers. What you say, how you act, and who you align with matters now more than ever. This is the time to manage your image like a professional.

In the next few chapters, we'll cover:

- How to evaluate NIL deals (not all money is good money)
- What to look for in a contract (and how to avoid getting played)
- How NIL income is taxed (yes, the IRS is watching)
- Why you should spread out your income to avoid tax traps
- How to think long-term instead of chasing fast cash
- Why your brand reputation is your new jersey number
- How to partner with the *right* people and avoid shady characters

We'll also talk about the people you need on your team: agents, CPAs, advisors, and trusted mentors like myself who are here to make sure you don't fumble the bag.

This Isn't Just About Money. It's About Legacy.

Anyone can make a quick check. Not everyone knows how to keep it, grow it, or build something bigger from it. NIL gives you the chance to do all three.

So as we step into this next part of your journey, I want you to keep one thing in mind:

NIL doesn't make you special—how you *handle* it does.

Let's help you shine in the spotlight—*without getting burned by it.* It's time to manage your NIL like a pro.

Chapter 3: NIL Income Running Your Own Offense

In every sport, the best offenses don't just rely on talent—they run plays with purpose. The quarterback doesn't snap the ball and just hope for the best. Every pass, every screen, every block is part of a strategy.

Now that you're earning money through NIL, it's your turn to run the offense.

This is your chance to call your own plays—not just on the field, but in life. The ball is in your hands. So the question is: what are you going to do with it?

What Is NIL Income, Really?

NIL income is any money you make from your Name, Image, or Likeness. It can come in different forms, including:

- Social media sponsorships
- Paid appearances or autograph signings
- Merchandise sales
- Endorsement deals
- YouTube monetization
- Personal brand partnerships

But no matter how you earn it, it's not free money. It's income. That means it's taxed, it needs to be tracked, and it needs to be managed like a business.

If you just start spending without a plan, you'll quickly find yourself playing from behind.

Every Check Is a Possession

Think of every NIL payment like a possession on offense. You have to decide:

- Do you score quickly (spend it)?
- Do you run clock (save it)?
- Do you set up a future play (invest it)?
- Or do you turn it over (spend recklessly and end up broke)?

Smart athletes play for four quarters, not just one. You need to think about what this money can do for you—not just today, but next month, next year, and even after your playing days are over.

Start With a Game Plan

Before you spend your first NIL dollar, ask yourself:

- How much should I set aside for taxes?
- What portion will I save?
- What's my monthly budget?
- What are my long-term financial goals?

This is where your financial playbook (budget) comes in. Without it, you're just calling audibles every play—and eventually, that'll catch up to you.

Don't Let NIL Control You—You Control It

It's easy to get caught up in the hype. You might see other athletes flashing new gear, trips, and luxuries online. But remember, not every highlight is the whole story. You don't know who's saving, who's broke, or who's going to owe thousands in taxes come April.

Run your offense based on your goals, not someone else's scoreboard.

You've trained your whole life to be disciplined in your sport. Apply that same discipline to your money. Make your NIL income work *for* you—not against you.

Final Word: Call Smart Plays

You're the quarterback now. NIL has given you the ball. Don't just run aimlessly. Have a plan. Know your routes. Trust your instincts. Protect your brand like it's the football—and lead your team (you and your future) to the end zone.

Run your NIL offense with confidence, clarity, and purpose—and you'll be scoring long after the season ends.

Analogy: NIL Deals Are Like Signing Endorsement Contracts — You're a Brand, Not Just a Baller

Let's talk facts: the minute you step into an NIL deal, you're not just an athlete—you're a brand.

Think about professional athletes like Serena Williams, Patrick Mahomes, or LeBron James. They don't just compete at the highest level—they partner with global brands, sign endorsement deals, and represent themselves like a business. Their name, image, and likeness hold value far beyond what they do on the court or field.

That's exactly what NIL is for you. When a company pays you to promote a product or show up for an event, they're not just supporting your athletic performance. They're investing in your personal brand. They're betting that your image, your voice, and your audience have enough influence to make people pay attention.

So let's break it down.

You're Not Just Playing—You're Representing

When you sign an NIL deal, it's like an endorsement contract. That company isn't just paying for a photo or a post—they're paying for what your name stands for.

That includes:

- How you present yourself online
- How you speak in public
- How you carry yourself in your sport
- What you post, share, like, and comment on
- The way you interact with teammates, fans, and even critics

Every action becomes part of your "brand tape." And just like a scout watches game film before offering a scholarship, brands are watching your personal highlight reel before offering a deal.

A Brand Has to Be Consistent

Let's say you're working with a local smoothie shop. You sign a deal, promote their product on your Instagram, wear their shirt, maybe even film a video at the store.

Then, the next day, you post something reckless online—something that doesn't align with the smoothie shop's values.

That brand may decide you're not worth the risk. They'll drop the deal. That's a contract fumble, and it happens more often than you think.

Being a brand means being intentional. You can still be yourself—authenticity matters—but now, you have to ask:

"Would I be proud of this post if a sponsor saw it?"

"Does this align with the type of partnerships I want to attract?"

Endorsements Are About Alignment, Not Just Money

The best NIL deals aren't just about the check. They're about alignment. When you partner with a brand that matches your values—whether that's healthy living, fashion, gaming, or community service—you're not just doing business. You're building credibility and long-term opportunities.

Think legacy, not likes. Think impact, not impulse.

Final Word: Protect Your Brand Like You Protect the Ball

Every NIL deal is a chance to build your business. So treat yourself like one. Be mindful. Be strategic. Be professional. And remember:

You're not just a baller—you're the CEO of your brand.

Make sure every deal you sign reflects that.

Read Contracts Carefully. Understand Terms Like...

You wouldn't sign a scholarship without knowing what you're agreeing to. You wouldn't commit to a team without understanding the coach's expectations. So why would you sign an NIL deal without reading the contract?

Contracts aren't just formalities—they're protection. They outline exactly what you're expected to do, what you're getting paid for, and what happens if something goes wrong. If you don't understand what's in them, you could end up locked into a bad deal, missing money, or damaging your eligibility and your brand.

Before you sign anything, make sure you understand these common NIL contract terms:

1. Deliverables

This is what you're agreeing to do.

- Are you expected to make Instagram posts?
- Wear their gear in public?
- Speak at an event or record a video?
- How many times? By what dates?

Know the "what," "when," and "how." If it's vague, ask for specifics. If it's confusing, don't be afraid to say, "Can you walk me through this?"

2. Compensation

How much are you getting paid—and how?

- Flat fee or recurring payments?
- Cash, gift cards, free products, or services?
- Is it paid upfront or after the deliverables are met?

Pro tip: Don't just look at the number. Look at the *value*. Free merchandise may sound great, but it won't help when rent is due.

3. Term (Length of Agreement)

How long does the deal last?

- One-time post or six months?
- Can you renew or cancel early?

Some brands try to lock you in long-term. That could block future, better deals. Short-term is often better unless it's a big opportunity.

4. Exclusivity

Are you restricted from working with competing brands?

If a protein company signs you, can you still promote other fitness brands? If you're exclusive, you can't accept similar deals elsewhere—even if they pay more.

Be careful here. Exclusivity limits your options.

5. Usage Rights

How can the brand use your image?

- Can they repost your content?
- Use your face in ads or on their website?
- Forever or just for a limited time?

Some contracts let companies use your name or content even after the deal ends. That's a big deal. Always ask how long they have the rights.

6. Termination Clause

How can the deal be ended?

- Can you back out if things go wrong?
- Can they cancel on you for a mistake or missed post?

You need to know what triggers cancellation—and whether you still get paid if the deal ends early.

Final Word: Know Before You Sign

NIL contracts are business deals. And in business, what you *don't* know can hurt you.

If something doesn't make sense, ask. Talk to a trusted adult, a compliance officer, an agent, or a financial advisor. Never let pressure or excitement push you into signing something you don't fully understand.

Because at the end of the day, your name is on that paper—and your future is on the line.

Exclusivity = Locked Into One Sponsor

Imagine this: You're a wide receiver having a breakout season. You've been working with a local clothing brand on some NIL deals—free gear, paid posts, and your own discount code. Then, a few months later, a bigger national brand reaches out. They want to offer you more money, better exposure, and a chance to be the face of a campaign.

But there's a problem.

You check your contract with the first brand and see a clause that says: "Exclusive Rights" or "Exclusivity." That means you've already agreed—whether you realized it or not—not to work with any similar companies while that deal is active.

And just like that, you're locked in. You can't take the better offer—even if it's 10x the money.

That's the power—and risk—of exclusivity.

What Does "Exclusivity" Really Mean?

In contract terms, exclusivity means you agree to only promote or work with one brand within a specific category for a set amount of time.

Here's how it might show up in a deal:

- "Athlete agrees not to endorse any competing energy drink or supple-

ment brand during the term of this agreement."
- "Brand retains exclusive rights to athlete's NIL for all footwear partnerships through [date]."

Even if it sounds casual or is buried deep in the fine print—it's binding. And if you break it, you could:

- Owe money back
- Lose the original deal
- Get sued (yes, really)
- Damage your brand reputation

It's Like Signing a Shoe Deal... at the Wrong Time

Think of it this way: A basketball player who signs with Nike can't turn around and wear Adidas next week. If you promote a hydration brand in September, and a competitor tries to offer you a better deal in October, you're stuck—if you didn't read or negotiate that exclusivity clause first.

So what do you do?

Smart Ways to Handle Exclusivity

1. Negotiate short-term exclusivity
2. Ask if the clause can be limited to just a few months, or even just the duration of the campaign. Don't lock up your NIL potential for a year over a single IG post.
3. Limit the category
4. Make sure the exclusivity only applies to a narrow lane (e.g., "protein powders") instead of the whole industry ("all sports nutrition").
5. Ask for more if they want exclusivity
6. If a brand wants to block other deals, you should be compensated more. You're giving up future opportunity—they should pay for that.
7. Have someone review the contract

8. A trusted advisor, NIL attorney, agent, who can help you spot exclusivity clauses before you're stuck.

Final Word: Know Before You Lock In

Exclusivity isn't always bad. In some cases, it can lead to strong partnerships. But if you don't read it carefully, you might be signing away more than just your time—you might be giving up future freedom.

So before you sign the dotted line, ask yourself:

Am I locking myself in too soon? Or am I keeping my options open to run my full playbook?

Termination Clauses = How You Can Get Dropped

In sports, every contract has an out. Whether it's a player getting cut from a team or a coach being let go mid-season, there's always a line in the agreement that explains how it can end. That's called a termination clause—and in your NIL deal, it's just as important as how much you're getting paid.

A termination clause spells out the conditions under which the deal can be canceled—either by the brand, by you, or by both parties. If you don't read this part carefully, you might think you have a six-month partnership... until you post one "off-brand" tweet and the company cuts ties instantly.

Let's break it down so you don't get blindsided.

What to Look for in a Termination Clause

Here are some common phrases you might see in a NIL termination clause:

- "This agreement may be terminated at any time by the sponsor for conduct deemed damaging to the brand."
- "Either party may terminate with 30 days' notice."
- "Breach of contract will result in immediate termination with no

compensation."

Now, think of that clause like a coach's reason to bench you.

If your effort drops, you violate team rules, or you act out—you're done. With NIL, it works the same way. Except instead of playing time, you lose the check, the brand relationship, and maybe your credibility.

Reasons NIL Deals Get Terminated

1. Conduct issues – Posting inappropriate content, getting into legal trouble, or behaving in a way the brand doesn't want to be associated with.
2. Missing deliverables – If you don't post on time, don't wear the gear, or don't show up to an appearance, you're in breach of contract.
3. Misrepresentation – If you exaggerate your stats, following, or engagement when signing the deal, and the brand finds out.
4. School or NCAA violations – If the deal jeopardizes your eligibility, the school might require the brand to terminate it.

How to Protect Yourself

Just like athletes have agents review their contracts before going pro, you need to read and understand the terms before signing anything.

Here's how to protect your bag:

- Ask: "What behavior could get me dropped?" You want to know what "conduct" the brand considers unacceptable.
- Ask: "Will I still get paid for work I've already done?" If you completed your deliverables before getting dropped, you should be compensated.
- Ask: "Can I terminate the contract if something changes?" You might want out if a better deal comes along, or if the brand doesn't hold up their end.
- Keep a paper trail. Save all emails, DMs, and deliverables just in case

the deal goes south and you need to protect yourself.

Final Word: Read the Fine Print Before You Sign the Deal

Just like you wouldn't want to get blindsided by a surprise cut from your team, you don't want to get dropped by a brand because you didn't understand the rules.

Read every clause. Ask questions. And remember: NIL isn't just about getting the deal—it's about keeping it.

Deliverables = What You're Required to Do

When you sign an NIL deal, you're not just getting a check for being an athlete—you're agreeing to do something in exchange for that money. That "something" is called a deliverable.

Think of deliverables as your assignments in the deal—just like your job on the field is to execute plays, your job in an NIL deal is to complete certain tasks the brand is paying you for.

Examples of Common Deliverables:

Deliverables can vary based on the deal, but here are some common ones:

- Social Media Posts: "Post three Instagram stories and one feed post tagging our brand using the hashtag #FueledByXYZ."
- Appearances: "Attend a one-hour meet-and-greet at our store."
- Product Usage: "Wear our gear in your TikToks and tag us once per week."
- Sponsored Content: "Create a 60-second video explaining why you love our product."
- Autographs or Signed Merchandise: "Sign 25 jerseys for promotional giveaways."

- Speaking Engagements: "Speak at our annual youth camp about your journey."

Some deliverables are super specific. Others are vague—and that's where problems happen.

Why Deliverables Matter So Much

If you don't know exactly what you've agreed to do, you could:

- Miss deadlines and violate the contract
- Do too much and get underpaid for your time
- Do too little and get dropped from the deal
- Accidentally break NCAA or school rules because you didn't clarify the details

Your NIL deal is a business agreement. Deliverables are your side of that agreement.

Questions to Ask Before Signing:

1. "What exactly am I required to do?" Ask for a clear, written list of deliverables: number of posts, events, dates, etc.
2.
3. "What platforms do I need to post on?" Instagram? TikTok? Twitter? YouTube? Your contract should say.
4. "Who provides the content—the brand or me?" Will you have to write your own captions, film your own videos, or will they send you a script or post template?
5. "What happens if I get injured, sick, or miss a deliverable?" Life happens. Make sure the contract has some flexibility.

Track Your Deliverables Like You Track Stats

Don't rely on memory. Create a simple checklist or calendar: Post 1 of 3 on Instagram

Tag brand in story

Attend Zoom promo event

Submit signed merchandise by [date]

Be a pro. Hit your deadlines. Communicate clearly.

Final Word: Treat Your Deliverables Like Your Job—Because They Are

You're not just getting paid because you're talented. You're getting paid to perform a service, just like a pro athlete fulfills obligations in a sponsorship deal.

When you deliver well, brands remember. That's how you build a reputation and open the door for even better NIL opportunities down the line.

So read the fine print, understand your deliverables, and get them done like the pro you're becoming.

Sample NIL Contract Breakdown (What to Look For and What It Means)

Before you sign any NIL agreement, you need to understand exactly what you're agreeing to. These aren't just handshake deals or friendly DMs—NIL contracts are legally binding agreements. That means what's written down matters more than what was said in a conversation.

Let's walk through a sample contract and break down what you should be looking for in each section:

1. Parties Involved

Sample: "This agreement is between Jayden Hill ('Athlete') and Peak

Performance Apparel, Inc. ('Sponsor')."

Make sure your full legal name is correct, and that the company you're working with is real and reputable. Look up the business, ask questions, and don't be afraid to research before signing.

2. Scope of Work (Deliverables)

Sample: "Athlete agrees to produce and publish two Instagram feed posts and three Instagram Stories featuring Sponsor's products over a 45-day campaign period."

This outlines what you're expected to do. How many posts? What kind of content? Are hashtags or tags required? Do you need to submit content for approval before posting? Make sure the details are clear.

3. Compensation

Sample: "Sponsor agrees to pay Athlete $1,500 upon completion of the deliverables."

What are you being paid? Is it cash, gift cards, free products, or something else? When will you be paid—upfront, halfway, or after the campaign ends? Don't just look at the number—understand the full value and payment schedule.

4. Term (Length of Agreement)

Sample: "This agreement shall remain in effect from April 1 through May 15."

This is how long the deal lasts. Make sure you know if you're signing up for a one-time post, a two-month campaign, or a year-long commitment. Avoid long-term contracts unless you're confident in the brand.

5. Exclusivity

Sample: "Athlete shall not enter into agreements with competing athletic apparel brands during the term of this agreement."

This means you can't work with certain other brands while this deal is active. Be clear on what counts as a "competing" brand. You could unknowingly block yourself from better opportunities later.

6. Termination Clause

Sample: "Sponsor may terminate this agreement immediately for conduct deemed inappropriate or damaging to the brand."

This section outlines the reasons either party can end the agreement early. What if you miss a post? What if they fail to pay you? Make sure both sides have accountability, and try to include a clause that protects you if something goes wrong.

7. Usage Rights

Sample: "Sponsor may use Athlete's name, image, and likeness for promotional use across all platforms for up to 12 months after the agreement ends."

This means the brand may continue using your content even after you've completed your part. Understand where and for how long your image can be used—and whether you're okay with it.

8. Taxes

Sample: "Athlete is solely responsible for all federal, state, and local taxes related to compensation received."

NIL income is taxable. The brand won't withhold taxes—you're responsible for setting money aside and paying what you owe. Plan to save at least 20–30% of what you earn.

Final Word

Always read the full contract. Highlight anything confusing. Ask questions. And if you're unsure, consult with a compliance officer, an NIL lawyer, or a trusted financial advisor.

You're not just signing a deal—you're running a business. Treat it that way.

Chapter 4: Taxes The Referees You Can't Ignore

Think of taxes like referees. They're not always front and center, but they're watching every play. And if you break the rules—even by accident—they'll throw a flag. Hard.

When it comes to NIL income, the IRS is the ultimate ref, and unlike game officials, they don't miss calls. They don't care how much you know (or don't know). If you're earning money, you owe taxes—period.

This chapter is your tax playbook. We're going to walk through what NIL money means for your taxes, how to prepare for it, and how to avoid penalties and surprises come April.

Why NIL Income Is Taxable

Let's be clear: NIL money is real money—and the government treats it like self-employment income. That means:

- No taxes are taken out when you get paid
- You're responsible for keeping track of your income
- You need to save a portion of your money for taxes (ideally 20–30%)

If you're thinking, *"But I didn't fill out any paperwork,"*—you probably did. Most NIL deals require a W-9 form before they pay you. That tells the company to issue you a 1099-NEC form at the end of the year, which reports your income to the IRS.

Common Forms You Might See

- W-9 – You fill this out before you get paid. It provides your name, address, and Social Security number or EIN.
- 1099-NEC – The brand sends you this form in January to report how much they paid you the year before.
- Schedule C – This is part of your tax return if you're self-employed (which NIL athletes often are).
- Schedule SE – This form calculates the self-employment tax you owe (an extra 15.3%).

How to Stay Ahead of the Game

1. Track every payment you receive
2. Use a spreadsheet, notes app, or accounting software. Record dates, amounts, and who paid you.
3. Set aside money for taxes as soon as you get paid
4. Best practice: move 25%–30% of each NIL check into a separate savings account labeled "Taxes." Don't touch it.
5. Consider paying quarterly estimated taxes
6. If you're making consistent NIL income, you may need to make payments four times a year. A CPA can help you calculate what's owed and when.
7. Save receipts and track expenses
8. If you use part of your NIL income for things like travel, marketing, or content creation, you may be able to deduct those costs on your taxes.

Get Professional Help

Unless you love numbers and tax law (and if you do—salute), don't try to do this alone. Hire a certified public accountant (CPA) who understands NIL income and self-employment taxes. Ask your school if they offer any free tax resources or access to financial professionals.

Final Word: Respect the Ref

Taxes might not be the most exciting part of NIL—but they're one of the most important. If you ignore them, they will catch up to you. And trust me, you do not want to play catch-up with the IRS.

So respect the referees. Learn the rules. Plan ahead. And keep your tax game tight—because winning off the field starts with being financially prepared.

Analogy: Not Understanding Taxes Is Like Not Knowing the Rules — You'll Lose Yards and Pay Penalties

Picture this: you're in a tight game, crowd's loud, it's 3rd and short—and your quarterback calls a perfect play. The ball snaps, you break free, pick up 15 yards… but then you hear it.

Flag on the field.

Illegal motion. The play gets called back. You lose five yards, the momentum is gone, and now it's 3rd and long.

That's what happens when you don't understand taxes.

You can be doing everything right—signing NIL deals, making money, building your brand—but if you don't know the rules of the tax game, it can all get called back. The IRS doesn't care how talented you are. They care whether you followed the rules. And if you don't? You'll lose ground. You'll pay penalties. And worst of all, you might owe more money than you have.

Let's be clear: not knowing isn't a free pass. Just like in sports, ignorance of the rules doesn't mean you're off the hook. If you don't set aside money for taxes, or if you don't file the right forms, you'll get flagged—and it'll cost you.

Common "Penalty Flags" for Student-Athletes

1. Not saving for taxes
2. You get a $5,000 NIL deal and spend all of it. Next spring, you find out you owe over $1,000 in taxes—and you don't have it.
3. Missing tax deadlines
4. Just like a delay of game, the IRS penalizes you for filing late. You can owe fees, interest, or both.
5. Not filing at all
6. This is the equivalent of walking off the field. If you earned income and didn't file taxes, the IRS will come looking—and the longer you wait, the worse it gets.
7. Filing incorrectly
8. Mess up your forms, forget to report income, or claim the wrong deductions? That's like lining up in the neutral zone. The play doesn't count, and now you're further behind.

Play Smart with a Game Plan

The same way you study film and know the playbook, you've got to study up on how your NIL income is taxed.

- Know what a 1099-NEC is and how to track it.
- Set aside a percentage of every check (aim for 25–30%) into a tax savings account.
- Hire a CPA or tax pro who understands NIL and self-employment income.
- Learn when to file quarterly estimated taxes, especially if you're earning consistently.

Just like in sports, a few small adjustments make a big difference. You don't have to master every tax rule—but you do have to respect the system.

Final Word: Know the Rules So You Don't Lose the Game

You wouldn't step onto the field without knowing the rules of your sport. So why would you step into the world of NIL income without understanding taxes?

Because at the end of the day, it doesn't matter how far you run or how many NIL deals you close—if the play gets called back for a penalty, it won't count.

Learn the rules. Respect the refs. Protect your progress. That's how you win both on and off the field.

Every NIL Dollar You Earn Is Taxable — No One's Taking Taxes Out for You

Let's keep it real: just because the check clears doesn't mean the money is all yours.

When you land your first NIL deal, whether it's $100 or $10,000, it's easy to get excited. You earned it. You posted the content, showed up to the event, or repped the brand like a pro. The money hits your account—and suddenly, you feel like you've arrived.

But before you spend a dime, understand this:

Every NIL dollar you earn is taxable. And unlike a regular job, no one's taking taxes out for you.

This is one of the most important financial lessons every student-athlete must learn. If you don't plan for taxes, they will catch up with you—and the IRS is not the kind of opponent you want to play from behind against.

Why This Happens

When you work a traditional job, like at a restaurant or summer gig, your employer takes taxes out of your paycheck before you even see it. That's W-2 income.

But when you earn money from NIL—whether it's from a brand partnership, appearance, or social media content—that money is considered self-employment income. You're the business now.

And as a business, you're responsible for setting aside your own taxes. The company paying you isn't going to do it for you. If they paid you $5,000, they expect you to figure out how much of that goes to taxes.

How Much Should You Set Aside?

A good rule of thumb is to save 25% to 30% of everything you earn. Here's how that breaks down:

- 10–12% for federal income tax
- 7.65% for self-employment tax (Social Security & Medicare)
- State taxes, depending on where you live and earn

So if you get a $1,000 NIL payment, set aside $250–$300 in a separate savings account labeled "TAXES." Do not touch it. Pretend it doesn't exist. That's not "extra" money—it's protection.

What Happens If You Don't Save?

Here's where most athletes get blindsided. You spend all your NIL money during the year... then in April, you get a 1099 form from the brand. The IRS sees it too. Now you owe $1,200—and you've got $50 in your account.

That's when penalties start piling up. Interest adds on. Stress kicks in. And suddenly, what felt like a big win becomes a financial mess.

Play Smart: Treat It Like a Business

- Track every dollar you earn from NIL
- Open a separate account to save for taxes
- Keep receipts for business-related expenses (you may be able to deduct them)
- Talk to a CPA or tax pro who can help you file correctly
- If you're making steady NIL income, consider paying quarterly estimated taxes so you're not hit with a huge bill all at once

Final Word: The IRS Doesn't Play

NIL is a blessing—but it comes with business responsibilities. Don't fall into the trap of thinking all your income is spendable. It's not.

Be smart. Save now. Stay ahead. Because no one's coming to do it for you—and this is one part of the game you *can't afford* to lose.

Tools Like TurboTax, H&R Block, or a Trusted CPA Help

Filing taxes doesn't have to be scary—but trying to do it alone, especially with NIL income, can get complicated fast. The good news? You don't have to figure it out by yourself.

There are tools and professionals out there designed to help you navigate tax season. Whether you're filing a simple return or reporting multiple NIL deals, getting help is one of the smartest plays you can make.

Option 1: TurboTax and H&R Block

TurboTax and H&R Block are two of the most popular tax prep tools for young adults, and both offer versions that walk you through every step of the filing process.

These platforms ask you basic questions (in plain English) about your income, expenses, and life situation—then automatically fill in the tax forms for you. At the end, they'll tell you whether you owe or are getting a refund.

You can even upload your 1099-NEC forms (the ones you'll receive from brands that paid you for NIL work), and the platform will know exactly how to handle them.

Why these tools are helpful:

- They're user-friendly and explain what you're doing as you go
- They catch mistakes and suggest deductions you might miss
- They're affordable (some versions are free or under $100)
- You can upgrade for live help from a tax pro if needed

If your NIL earnings were limited and your finances are pretty simple, these tools are a great place to start.

Option 2: A Trusted CPA (Certified Public Accountant)

If you made more money through NIL, signed multiple contracts, or had different types of income (like YouTube ads, merchandise sales, or brand collabs), then it might be worth working with a real tax professional—a CPA.

A CPA is like your tax coach. They know how the game works, they keep up with the rulebook, and they'll help you avoid costly mistakes. They can also help you:

- Calculate how much you owe
- File your taxes correctly and on time
- Set up quarterly payments if you need them
- Track your deductions (travel, marketing, business expenses)
- Plan ahead for next year's tax strategy

Working with a CPA costs more than using an app—but it's often worth it if your NIL business is growing. You might even save more on taxes than what you pay for their help.

Where to Find Help:

- Ask your university if they offer access to free or discounted tax prep services for athletes
- Search for CPAs who specialize in working with small businesses or self-employed individuals
- Reach out to someone, who works with student-athletes and understands NIL income

Final Word: Get the Help You Need

You wouldn't try to draw up a defensive scheme without your coach—and you shouldn't try to do taxes solo if you're unsure. Use the tools. Ask the questions. Hire the help.

Because the goal isn't just to get through tax season—it's to get through it clean, confident, and in control of your financial future.

Sample IRS Forms: W-9, 1099-NEC, Schedule C

If you're earning money through NIL (Name, Image, and Likeness), you're officially in business—and that means the IRS expects you to report your income and file taxes like a self-employed entrepreneur.

But don't panic—once you know what forms to expect, it's easier to stay on top of it. Here are the three most common IRS forms you'll deal with as a student-athlete earning NIL income:

1. W-9 Form: The Pre-Game Setup

What it is:

The W-9 is the form a company asks you to fill out before they pay you. It collects your basic info: name, address, and Social Security number (or Tax ID number, if you have one).

Why it matters:

The W-9 tells the brand you're working with how to report your income to the IRS. Once you submit a W-9, they'll send you a 1099 form the following January to show how much they paid you.

When you'll see it:

Usually before you get paid. If a brand doesn't ask for one, that doesn't mean you don't owe taxes—it just means they might not be handling their end properly.

What to do:

Fill it out carefully. Make sure your info matches your legal records. Save a copy for your own files.

2. 1099-NEC Form: The Stat Sheet

What it is:

This form shows how much money you were paid by a company in a calendar year as a non-employee. It's like your NIL income stat sheet.

Why it matters:

Any company that pays you $600 or more in a year is legally required to send you a 1099-NEC form by January 31 of the following year. You must report that amount on your taxes—even if you weren't sent the form.

When you'll see it:

You'll receive one from each brand or company that paid you more than $600.

What to do:

Collect all your 1099s. Compare them to your records to make sure everything matches. You'll use these forms to file your taxes.

3. Schedule C: Your Business Playbook

What it is:

Schedule C is part of your tax return. It reports your income and expenses from self-employment (which includes NIL deals).

Why it matters:

This is where you show how much you made *and* how much you spent running your "business"—which could include things like:

- Travel to events
- Marketing expenses
- Website fees
- Equipment used for content creation

These expenses can reduce how much tax you owe, legally and responsibly.

When you'll see it:

You or your CPA will fill out a Schedule C as part of your annual tax filing.

What to do:

Track your income and expenses throughout the year so your Schedule C is accurate and you're ready at tax time.

Final Word: These Forms Are Part of the Game

Being in the NIL world means handling real money—and real money means real paperwork. Knowing how these forms work helps you stay ahead of the IRS, avoid surprises, and build your financial foundation like a pro.

You're not just an athlete anymore. You're a business. And businesses file their paperwork.

Pro Tip: Spread Income Over Multiple Years to Lower Tax Hits

Let's talk strategy—not just on the field, but with your money.

One of the smartest moves you can make with NIL income is to spread it out over time instead of taking it all at once. Why? Because the more you earn in a single year, the higher your tax bracket can go—and the more you'll owe the IRS.

This is a tip even many adults miss: it's not just how much you make—it's when you make it.

Why Spreading Income Matters

The U.S. tax system is progressive, meaning the more you make, the higher the percentage you're taxed on the *next* dollar you earn. So, if you earn $40,000 in one year from NIL and nothing the next, you might get taxed in a higher bracket than if you earned $20,000 two years in a row.

By spreading income over multiple years, you:

- Stay in a lower tax bracket
- Owe less in taxes overall
- Have more time to plan, save, and invest

This is especially useful if you're signing multi-post or multi-month NIL deals, where you can negotiate when and how you're paid.

Example: All at Once vs. Spread Out

Scenario 1: All at once

You get a big NIL deal and the company pays you $30,000 in October. You're taxed on all of that income in the current calendar year—even though you only had three months to use it or plan for taxes.

Scenario 2: Spread out

You ask the company to split the payments into two parts—$15,000 this year and $15,000 next year. Now, you cut your annual tax burden, may avoid jumping tax brackets, and have time to save and prepare.

The brand gets their deliverables either way—you just negotiated a smarter payout schedule.

How to Make It Happen

1. Negotiate payment terms up front
2. When reviewing your NIL contract, ask if the compensation can be spread over time instead of paid in a lump sum.

3. Work with a CPA or tax advisor
4. A professional can help you model different scenarios to see what makes the most sense for your income level and goals.
5. Don't rush to cash the check
6. Sometimes it's smarter to take less now and more later. Think long-term—not short-term hype.
7. Plan your deliverables accordingly
8. Make sure your deliverables are aligned with the payment schedule. Brands don't want to pay you before they get what they're paying for.

Final Word: Think Like a Business Owner

This is the kind of tax move that separates the amateurs from the pros. You're not just collecting checks—you're managing a financial future.

Spreading your NIL income out doesn't mean earning less—it means keeping more. That's what smart businesses do. And now that you're one? It's time to play the long game.

Save money, lower your tax bill, and build financial habits that last way beyond your playing days.

Part 3: Investing – Your Financial Training Program

As an athlete, you understand what it takes to succeed—discipline, reps, and long-term commitment. You don't just walk into the weight room once and expect to get stronger. You train day in and day out because you know the results come later.

Investing works the same way.

You may not see the results overnight. But if you start early, stay consistent, and follow the game plan, your money can grow and work for you—long after your playing days are over. That's what this part of the book is about: turning the NIL money you're earning today into long-term financial wins tomorrow.

This is your financial training program—and just like any great workout plan, it starts with the fundamentals.

Why Investing Matters Now

Most people don't think about investing until they're older—but that's a mistake. The earlier you start, the more time your money has to grow through compound interest. It's like putting your money in the weight room and letting it get stronger all by itself.

Here's the magic: If you invest just $100 a month starting in college, by the time you're 40, that could grow into tens of thousands of dollars—without you doing anything but staying consistent.

And if you set aside a portion of your NIL income now? You're building financial muscle that'll carry you for decades.

What You'll Learn in This Section

We're going to break down the essentials of investing—no confusing jargon, no Wall Street talk. Just real, simple information to help you grow your money like a pro.

In the next few chapters, you'll learn:

- How investing is like preparing for the playoffs—slow gains over time lead to big wins
- The difference between stocks, bonds, index funds, and crypto
- How to open your first investment account or Roth IRA
- Why investing isn't the same as gambling (and how to tell the difference)
- How to avoid get-rich-quick schemes that prey on athletes
- Real stories of athletes who invested smart—and others who didn't
- How to work with a financial advisor, and what questions to ask

This Is Bigger Than NIL

Investing isn't just for people who go pro or make millions. It's for anyone who wants freedom. Options. Control. Whether you end up starting your own business, working a 9-to-5, or making it to the league—the financial decisions you make now can set you up for life.

Just like training, there will be some soreness at the beginning. It might feel confusing or uncomfortable. But the more reps you put in, the more confident you'll get.

Final Word: Train Your Money Like You Train Your Body

This is your financial gym. Your NIL money is your fuel. And investing is how you build lasting strength.

Let's get into it—and start turning today's earnings into tomorrow's wealth. Because the best athletes don't just play the game—they invest in the future.

Chapter 5: Investing 101 Let Your Money Train Too

You spend hours every week training your body. You work on your speed, your strength, your stamina—because you know it pays off when game time comes. But there's one thing a lot of athletes overlook:

Your money needs training too.

Just like your muscles grow with reps and time, your money grows through something called compound interest—the most powerful force in the financial world. And the earlier you start investing, the stronger your financial future becomes.

So let's break it down. No fancy finance degree required. Just like your first day in the weight room, we're starting with the basics and building up.

What Is Investing, Really?

Investing is when you put your money into something—like stocks, bonds, or mutual funds—with the goal of helping it grow over time. You're not just saving; you're giving your money a job.

Think of it like hiring a trainer for your money. While you're focused on your sport, your dollars are out there doing squats, sprint work, and film study—gaining value behind the scenes.

Why You Should Start Now (Even With a Little)

You don't need thousands of dollars to begin. You just need consistency and time.

Let's say you invest $100 a month starting at age 20. By the time you're 40, that could grow to over $60,000–$80,000 or more, depending on how the market performs. That's without doing anything extra—just small, consistent deposits.

If you wait until age 30 to start, that same monthly $100 might only grow to half as much by age 40. Time is your biggest asset—use it now.

Where Can You Invest?

- Roth IRA: A great place to start. You invest post-tax dollars, and your money grows tax-free. That means when you retire, you don't pay taxes on your earnings. Most student-athletes qualify.
- Brokerage Account: Like an online locker for your investments. Apps like Fidelity, Vanguard, Schwab, or Robinhood let you start with small amounts and buy stocks or funds.
- Index Funds & ETFs: Instead of picking individual stocks, these bundle many stocks together so you can invest in a wide range of companies (like the entire S&P 500) with less risk.

Don't Confuse Investing With Gambling

Buying meme stocks, chasing hype on TikTok, or throwing everything into crypto without research? That's not investing—that's speculating.

Real investing is:

- Long-term focused
- Diversified (spreading your money across different assets)
- Based on goals, not emotion
- Boring sometimes—and that's a good thing

You wouldn't skip training because it wasn't exciting, right? The same goes for building wealth.

Final Word: Train Now, Flex Later

If you can commit to showing up for practice, sticking to a training plan, and trusting the process in sports, you already have what it takes to be a great investor.

Let your money train too. Start now, even if it's just a little. Stay consistent. Play the long game.

Because your future self—the one not worrying about money at 40—will thank you for the reps you're putting in today.

Analogy: Investing Is Like Strength Training – Results Come from Consistency, Not One Big Lift

Let's take it to the weight room.

Imagine walking into the gym for the first time and throwing 315 pounds on the bench press. No warm-up. No foundation. Just going all in on Day 1. Not only are you likely to fail—you could get hurt, discouraged, or walk away thinking strength training "doesn't work."

That's how a lot of people treat investing.

They think they have to wait until they have a ton of money, then dump it all in the market at once. Or they try to make a huge score on a single "hot stock," expecting overnight results. But real strength—and real wealth—isn't built in one session. It's built over time.

Investing is like strength training. You make the most progress by showing up consistently, doing the reps, and letting time do its job.

The Power of Small, Consistent Reps

You don't get strong by lifting once a month. You build strength by doing something small every day or every week. It's the same with investing.

Even investing $50 or $100 a month can grow into something powerful over time, especially when you start young. The key is consistency—not perfection, not timing the market, not chasing the next big thing.

That $100 a month might not seem like much now, but over 10, 15, or 20 years, it turns into serious money thanks to compound interest—the financial equivalent of progressive overload in the gym.

You Don't Need to Be a Pro to Start

Just like you don't need to be a powerlifter to begin working out, you don't need to be a financial expert to start investing.

You don't need to know how to "pick stocks" or follow the news every day. You just need to:

- Open an investment account (like a Roth IRA or brokerage account)
- Start with a small amount
- Invest in simple, reliable options like index funds or ETFs
- Add to it regularly—even if it's just a little

And just like training, the hardest part is showing up early on. Once the habit is in place, the process takes over.

Ignore the Noise, Trust the Program

Some days, you'll feel like skipping the gym. Some weeks, your lifts won't go up. But if you stay the course, you'll get stronger.

Same with investing. The market will have ups and downs. Some months your money will grow fast. Other months, it might dip. But if you stick to the plan, keep contributing, and don't panic, you'll build wealth steadily and safely—just like building strength one rep at a time.

Final Word: Lift for the Life You Want

You're already training your body and your mind. Now it's time to train your money.

Investing isn't about one big win—it's about consistent reps over time.

Show up. Stay patient. Do the work.

Because when your money gets stronger, your future does too.

Open a Roth IRA or Brokerage Account — Here's How

Now that you're earning money through NIL, you're in the perfect position to take a major step toward long-term wealth: investing. And two of the best places to start are a Roth IRA and a brokerage account.

Think of these like your lockers for wealth-building. You put money in, let it work out behind the scenes, and years from now—you unlock serious results.

Let's break it down.

Step 1: Know the Difference

Roth IRA

- Best for retirement
- Contributions are made with *after-tax* money
- Money grows tax-free
- You can withdraw your contributions (not earnings) anytime
- Max contribution: $6,500/year (as of 2024, if you earn income)

Brokerage Account

- Flexible for general investing (not just retirement)

- No contribution limits
- Can invest in stocks, ETFs, index funds, etc.
- You'll owe taxes on earnings and dividends

Which one first?

If you qualify, start with a Roth IRA because of the long-term tax benefits. If you want more flexibility or already maxed out your Roth, open a brokerage account.

Step 2: Choose a Platform

Pick a trusted investment company or app. Here are some beginner-friendly options:

- Fidelity (great for both Roth IRAs and brokerage accounts)
- Charles Schwab (excellent service and no account minimums)
- Vanguard (ideal for long-term, low-cost investing)
- E*TRADE, Robinhood, or SoFi (more app-based and user-friendly, but do your research)

Look for platforms with:

- No account minimums
- No trading fees on stocks or ETFs
- Strong mobile app and customer support

Step 3: Gather What You Need

Before opening your account, have this info ready:

- Social Security number
- Legal name, address, and date of birth
- Bank account info (to fund your investments)

- Employer info (if asked; just list NIL/self-employed if that's your income)

Step 4: Open Your Account (Takes 15–20 Minutes)

Go to your chosen platform's website or app and follow the prompts to open a:

- Roth IRA (if you've earned income this year)
- Or a Brokerage Account (if you want flexibility or additional investing)

You'll be asked to:

- Verify your identity
- Choose your account type
- Set up funding (how much to deposit now or monthly)
- Select investments (you can start with an index fund like S&P 500 ETF or ask a professional)

Pro tip: If you're not sure what to invest in yet, you can fund the account but wait to invest. Just don't let that money sit for too long doing nothing.

Step 5: Automate It and Forget It

Once the account is set up, set a monthly auto-deposit (even $50–$100). This is your financial workout plan—small consistent reps that build long-term wealth.

Final Word: Start Small, Think Big

Opening a Roth IRA or brokerage account is a major move toward financial independence. Most college students don't do this—but you're not most students.

Start early. Be consistent. Let your money grow while you're chasing greatness on and off the field.

Because one day, your future self will thank you for opening that account today.

Analogy: Stocks, Bonds, and ETFs = Your Reps, Sets, and Programs

When you're in the weight room, you don't just do one exercise and call it a day. You mix it up—different reps, sets, and training programs depending on your goal. Some days you lift heavy. Some days you focus on recovery. All of it builds toward one thing: total strength.

Investing works the same way. And in your financial workout, stocks, bonds, and ETFs are your tools—the reps, sets, and structured programs that build wealth over time.

Let's break it down.

Your Heavy Lifts (High-Reward Reps)

When you buy a stock, you're buying a small piece of a company—like Apple, Nike, or Amazon. If that company grows, so does your investment. Stocks can give you strong returns over time, but they also come with more risk (just like lifting heavy weight—you can make gains, but you can also get hurt if your form's off).

Why it's like a heavy lift:

- More potential reward
- Requires confidence and consistency
- Can be volatile—ups and downs are normal
- Best when part of a bigger, balanced routine

Pro tip: Don't go all in on one stock. Diversify, just like you wouldn't only bench press and skip legs. Mix it up.

Bonds = Your Recovery Days (Safe, Steady Sets)

Bonds are like the stretching and recovery work in your training. They're lower risk, offer consistent returns, and help protect your money. When you buy a bond, you're basically lending money to a company or government in exchange for regular interest payments.

Why it's like a recovery day:

- Slower growth, but steady
- Low risk
- Keeps your overall routine balanced
- Helps protect your portfolio from burnout (aka market crashes)

You may not feel like you're getting stronger on those lighter days, but they matter in the long run. Same with bonds.

ETFs = Your Workout Programs (Pre-Built Plans)

ETFs (Exchange-Traded Funds) are like structured workout plans. Instead of picking individual stocks or bonds, ETFs bundle them together so you can invest in hundreds of companies at once.

There are ETFs for all kinds of goals—like the S&P 500 ETF (invests in the top 500 U.S. companies), dividend ETFs (for income), or sector ETFs (tech, energy, sportswear, etc.).

Why it's like a workout program:

- Built-in structure and balance
- Less thinking, more doing
- Easy to stick with long-term
- Great for beginners and pros

ETFs are one of the best places to start if you're new to investing. You get instant diversification without needing to know everything.

Final Word: Build Your Financial Fitness Plan

Just like a complete training program includes strength, mobility, and recovery—a good investment plan includes stocks, bonds, and ETFs. Each plays a role. Each helps you grow.

So start where you are. Pick your reps. Stick to the program. And remember:

The weight you lift today turns into wealth tomorrow—if you stay consistent.

Compound Interest Is Your Gains-Over-Time Chart: $200/Month in Your Early 20s Can Be Over $300K by Age 50

You already understand progress over time. You've seen it in the gym, on the field, and in the classroom. You didn't get stronger, faster, or better overnight—it took reps, discipline, and belief in the process.

Now imagine your money doing the same thing.

That's the power of compound interest—the financial version of progressive overload. It's how your money grows not just on what you put in, but also on what it's already earned. Over time, it builds momentum. It's like your gains compounding month after month, year after year.

And here's the part most people miss: starting early makes all the difference.

The Math Behind the Magic

Let's say you start investing just $200 a month at age 22. That's $2,400 a year—about the cost of a new phone or a couple nights out per month.

If you invest that consistently in a basic index fund earning an average return of 8% per year, by the time you're 50, you could have over $300,000.

You will have contributed $67,200 of your own money over 28 years...

But you'll have gained over $230,000 in interest alone.

That's compound interest doing the heavy lifting—your money training itself.

Now, imagine if you waited until age 30 to start. Same $200/month, same returns, but now you've got 8 fewer years. You'll only have around $180,000 instead of $300,000.

That's a $120,000 difference—just for starting early.

Why Compound Interest Works So Well

Compound interest is powerful because:

- Your earnings get reinvested automatically
- Your money earns interest on top of interest
- Time multiplies everything—like adding more plates to the bar over time

It's like turning your savings into a snowball. At first, it rolls slow and small. But over time, it picks up speed—and suddenly it's massive and rolling on its own.

What You Can Do Now

1. Open a Roth IRA or brokerage account
2. Start investing—even if it's just $50 or $100/month.
3. Be consistent

4. Set up automatic deposits, so you don't even have to think about it.
5. Reinvest your earnings
6. Let your dividends and gains roll right back into your investments—no withdrawals.
7. Stay patient
8. There will be ups and downs in the market. Don't panic. Stay in the game.

Final Word: Time Is Your Teammate

You train your body because you know it will pay off later. Treat your money the same way.

Compound interest is your gains-over-time chart. You won't see results right away, but the longer you stick with it, the bigger the growth.

Start now. Be consistent. Let your money get in shape—and watch it build strength while you sleep.

Because a few smart moves in your 20s can mean total financial freedom in your 40s and 50s. That's the real win.

Sample Investment Statements + How to Read Them Included

Once you start investing—whether in a Roth IRA or a brokerage account—you'll begin receiving monthly or quarterly investment statements. These reports show you how your money is performing, what you own, and where your account stands.

At first glance, these statements might look like they're written in a foreign language. But don't worry—reading an investment statement is easier than reading a playbook once you know the basics.

Let's break it down using a simple, sample layout:

Sample Investment Statement – What to Look For

Here's what a typical investment statement includes:

1. Account Summary

This is your quick snapshot.

Example:

- Beginning Balance (Jan 1): $2,000
- Contributions: $200
- Investment Gains/Losses: +$80
- Ending Balance (Jan 31): $2,280

This section tells you how your money moved over the statement period—did your account grow, shrink, or stay the same?

What to look for:

- Are your automatic deposits showing up?
- Is your account balance growing over time?

2. Holdings (What You Own)

This section lists all the investments in your account.

Example:

Investment Name

Type

Shares

Value

% of Portfolio

Vanguard S&P 500 ETF

ETF

5.2

$2,080

91%

Cash

Money Mkt

—

$200

9%

What to look for:

- What types of investments do you have? (Stocks, ETFs, bonds, cash)
- Are you diversified?
- Is most of your money invested, or just sitting in cash?

3. Performance Summary
This shows how your account has performed over time.
Example:

- Month-to-date: +4.0%
- Year-to-date: +7.5%
- Since inception: +8.2%

What to look for:

- Am I gaining or losing money?
- How does my return compare to the overall market?

Don't stress about short-term dips. Investing is a long game. Focus on steady progress over months and years—not day-to-day changes.

4. Transactions
This shows everything that happened in your account.
Example:

- Jan 5: Auto deposit +$200
- Jan 6: Bought 0.5 shares of Vanguard S&P 500 ETF

- Jan 20: Dividend reinvested +$5.24

What to look for:

- Are your deposits and investments being made properly?
- Are dividends being reinvested (this helps compound your growth)?
- Are there any unexpected fees?

How to Read It Like a Pro

- Green = Growth: If your balance is increasing and gains are showing, your money's working.
- Track Contributions: Know what *you* added versus what the *market* earned.
- Monitor Costs: Check for any hidden fees or account maintenance charges.

Ask Questions: If you don't understand something, call the investment platform or talk to a financial advisor.

Final Word: Learn the Language of Wealth

An investment statement is like your financial stat sheet. The more you understand it, the better you can make smart decisions.

Start simple. Review your statement each month. Celebrate growth. Adjust if needed. And remember—this is your financial progress report, and you're in control.

Chapter 6: Car Chase

This is soooo random, I always wanted to write a book with a car chase! Any time someone tells me about a book—whether it's a mystery, romance, financial guide, or even a cookbook—I always ask with a smile:

"But does it have a car chase?"

So YES, this book even has a Car Chase!

It's my way of saying: is there *movement*? Is there *action*? Is there something that makes it exciting?

So yes—this book absolutely has a car chase.

But not in the Fast & Furious way (although, if Vin Diesel wants to narrate the audiobook, let's talk). No, this car chase is the one you're already in… right now. It's the wild, high-speed pursuit called Name, Image, and Likeness.

You're the driver.

You've got talent, visibility, and momentum.

The engine's running, the opportunity is real, and the road ahead is wide open.

But let's talk about your dashboard for a second.

Are you watching your fuel—aka your budget? Because too many student-athletes run hot with NIL money and burn through it before the first season ends.

Is your check engine light on? That might be that contract you didn't fully read. Or the taxes you haven't set aside. Or that cousin who keeps asking for "just a little help."

Are you checking your rearview mirror? Because behind you are people trying to catch up—maybe even catch you slipping. The IRS, compliance offices, scammers, and old spending habits don't just disappear when the money comes in.

And what about your GPS? Are you actually headed toward something—like long-term wealth, entrepreneurship, or financial freedom—or are you just taking exits that look cool in the moment?

This NIL car chase isn't about speed. It's about control.

It's about knowing when to shift gears, when to pull over and get help, and when to hit the gas.

Yes, people are going to zoom past you on social media. They'll flash deals, big purchases, and rented lifestyles. But what they won't post are the breakdowns, the burnout, and the "out of gas" moments that come when you drive with no plan.

So here's your moment to shift. To get in the driver's seat with clarity, confidence, and a clean dashboard.

This book is your manual. Your map. Your mechanic in the glovebox.

Because NIL is fast. Life is faster. And trust me—there's no worse feeling than realizing you had the keys to your own success, but never learned how to drive it.

So yeah, this book has a car chase.

And you? You're the one steering. Let's make sure you know where you're going.

Chapter 7: Understanding Your Investment Statement

When you invest, your money isn't just sitting—it's working. And just like you track your stats after a game or check your progress in the gym, you need to track your financial performance too. That's where your investment statement comes in.

At first glance, these documents might look complicated or boring. But once you learn to read them, you'll realize they're actually your financial highlight reel—showing what your money's doing, where it's going, and how it's growing.

Let's walk through how to read your investment statement like a pro.

What Is an Investment Statement?

An investment statement is a report from your brokerage or Roth IRA provider (like Fidelity, Vanguard, or Charles Schwab). It's usually sent monthly or quarterly and shows:

- How much money you've contributed
- How much your investments have grown or dropped
- What you actually own in your account
- Any dividends or gains you've received

Think of it like a stat sheet that tells the full story of your money's performance.

Key Sections to Understand

1. Account Summary
   This is your scoreboard.
   It shows:

   - Beginning balance (how much was in your account at the start)
   - New contributions (how much you added this month/quarter)
   - Investment gains or losses
   - Ending balance (your current total)

This gives you a big-picture view: Is your account going up or down? Is your money working? Are you contributing consistently?

2. Holdings or Portfolio Breakdown
   This is your lineup.
   It shows what your money is invested in—like:

   - Stocks (Apple, Nike, Amazon)
   - ETFs (like an S&P 500 fund)
   - Bonds
   - Cash or money market funds

It also tells you how much each investment is worth and what percentage it makes up of your total portfolio.

Why it matters: You want to be diversified, not all-in on one company or investment type. That's how you protect yourself from risk.

3. Performance Summary
   This is your stat tracker over time.
   You'll see:

- Month-to-date performance
- Year-to-date returns
- Since-you-started growth

This helps you understand whether your money is trending in the right direction. And remember: Investing is a long game. Don't panic over short-term dips—focus on the big picture.

4. Transactions History
   This is your play-by-play.
   It shows:

- Deposits or contributions
- Purchases of new investments
- Reinvested dividends
- Fees (if any)

Make sure your contributions and reinvestments are happening as planned. If anything looks off, contact your provider immediately.

Tips for Reviewing Your Statement

- Check it once a month like you check your training logs
- Focus on progress over time, not daily ups and downs
- If you don't understand a section, ask questions—your money is too important to guess on
- Use your statement to adjust your goals and contributions

Final Word: Know Your Numbers, Own Your Future

Understanding your investment statement is like studying film—you learn what's working, where to improve, and how to win long-term.

You're building something big. Reading your statement each month keeps you in control, keeps you informed, and keeps your money moving forward.

Because smart athletes track more than their stats—they track their wealth too.

Think of It Like a Post-Game Stat Sheet. Learn:

After every game, you check the box score, right? You want to know how many points you scored, how many assists you dished out, what your shooting percentage was, or how many tackles you made. That stat sheet tells your performance story—what you did right, where you need to improve, and how you impacted the game.

Well, your investment statement is your financial stat sheet. It tells you how your money performed, how consistent you've been, and whether you're trending in the right direction over time. Learning how to read it is just as important as reviewing game film or lifting stats—it's how you grow financially.

Let's break down what you should be looking for, just like you would in a post-game review.

1. Your Contributions (How Much You Played)

Just like minutes played in a game tell you how much you were on the court, your contributions show how much you're showing up financially.

Check:

- How much did you add this month?
- Are you making regular contributions?
- Are your automatic deposits hitting your account?

Consistency matters. You don't need to drop 30 every night, but showing up regularly builds results—on the court *and* in your portfolio.

2. Your Growth (What You Scored)

This section shows how much your investments gained (or lost) during the statement period. It's like seeing how many points you scored, or whether you helped your team win.

Check:

- Did your balance grow from interest, dividends, or market returns?
- Are your gains steady, or are you seeing big swings?

Don't stress over short-term losses. Even LeBron has an off night. What matters is that, over the season (and career), your numbers go up.

3. Your Holdings (Your Role on the Team)

This tells you what you're actually invested in. Think of it like your position and responsibilities on the squad. Are you carrying too much weight in one area (like all your money in one stock)? Or are you well-balanced, with investments spread across different areas?

Check:

- What percentage is in stocks, bonds, ETFs, or cash?
- Are you diversified, or overly focused on one type of asset?

Diversification is like having a strong bench. If one player struggles, the team keeps moving.

4. Your Transactions (What Plays You Ran)

This shows your financial playbook: deposits, purchases, reinvestments, or withdrawals. It helps you track whether the game plan is being executed.

Check:

- Are your recurring deposits showing up?
- Are you reinvesting dividends?
- Any surprise fees or deductions?

Just like you review tape to see what worked, reviewing this helps you make better financial decisions next quarter.

Final Word: Study Your Stats

Don't just let your investment statement sit unread in your inbox. Study it like film. Break it down like a box score.

Because the more you understand what your money is doing, the better decisions you can make next month, next year, and for your future.

This is your financial game tape—and you're the star of the show.

Asset Allocation = Offensive/Defensive Balance

In sports, a great team doesn't win by focusing only on offense or only on defense—it takes balance. You need scorers who can light it up, and defenders who can shut things down. The same goes for your investments.

Asset allocation is your financial version of that game plan. It's how you divide your money between different types of investments—some aggressive (offense), some conservative (defense). And getting the right balance can help you grow your money over time while protecting it from getting wiped out during market downturns.

Let's break it down in your language.

Offense = Growth Assets (Stocks)

Stocks are the players that put points on the board. They have the most potential to grow your money over time—but they can also be unpredictable.

- Examples: Individual stocks, growth ETFs, sector funds (like tech or emerging markets)
- Role: Help you build long-term wealth
- Risk: Higher. Stocks can go up fast—but also drop during bad market years

Offensive players take bold shots and make headlines. Same with stocks. They drive most of your long-term growth, but they can't carry the team alone.

Defense = Stability Assets (Bonds, Cash, CDs)

Defense wins championships—and in your investment portfolio, defensive assets protect you when the market gets rough. They don't usually grow as fast as stocks, but they hold steady and give your money structure.

- Examples: Bonds, Treasury bills, money market funds, high-yield savings
- Role: Reduce risk, protect your account from big losses
- Risk: Lower. These investments don't jump much in value—but they don't fall as hard either

Think of these as your lockdown defenders. They won't lead in scoring, but when your offense struggles, they hold the line.

Asset Allocation = Building the Right Team

When you decide how much of your money to put into stocks (offense) versus bonds/cash (defense), you're making an asset allocation decision.

There's no one-size-fits-all formula, but here are some starting points:

- Aggressive (80% offense, 20% defense): You're young, have time, and can handle the ups and downs of the market. Great for student-athletes

starting early.
- Moderate (60/40 or 70/30): You want growth, but also some safety.
- Conservative (40% offense, 60% defense): You're close to needing the money or want to reduce risk.

Just like in sports, the right mix depends on your goals, risk tolerance, and time horizon.

Final Word: Build a Balanced Playbook

You wouldn't put five scorers on the floor with no defense. And you wouldn't go into a game with all defense and no offense.

Your investments need the same balance.

Asset allocation is how you build a well-rounded portfolio that grows over time and stays strong when the economy gets shaky. It's your financial Xs and Os.

So draft your financial team wisely—because in the long run, the win goes to the investors who know how to balance scoring big with protecting the lead.

Performance = Your Record Over Time

In sports, your record says a lot.

It tells people how you've performed over the season—not just in one game, but over weeks, months, and the entire schedule. You might have had an off night or a tough matchup, but if you stayed consistent and kept improving, your record reflects that growth.

Your investment performance works the same way.

It's not about how your money does in one week or one month—it's about how it performs over time. Performance is your financial win-loss record. It tells you whether you're moving in the right direction, sticking to your game plan, and making steady progress toward your goals.

What Is Investment Performance?

Investment performance measures how much your investments have grown—or dropped—over a certain period. Most investment statements will show your:

- Month-to-date return
- Year-to-date (YTD) return
- One-year, three-year, and five-year performance
- "Since inception" performance (since you opened the account)

This tells you how your portfolio is doing overall. Just like you wouldn't judge a season by one quarter, you shouldn't judge your investments by one bad day in the market.

Short-Term vs. Long-Term Performance

Let's say your account drops 2% in one month. That might feel like a loss—but if your year-to-date return is still +8%, you're actually winning the long game.

Investing isn't a sprint—it's a season. The key is to focus on trends, not temporary swings.

Think of it like this:

- One bad game? No big deal.
- A losing streak? Time to review the strategy.
- A winning record over the long run? That's the goal.

What Impacts Your Performance?

Several factors influence how your investments perform:

- Market conditions (the economy, interest rates, inflation)

- Your asset allocation (mix of stocks, bonds, ETFs, etc.)
- Your consistency (how often you invest)
- How early you started (time in the market = major advantage)

Some of these things are out of your control—just like referees or weather conditions. What matters most is that you stick to your game plan and stay in the game.

How to Review Your Performance

Once a month or quarter, look at your investment statement and ask:

- Has my total balance grown over time?
- Am I contributing consistently?
- How has my account done year-to-date?
- Is my asset mix helping me grow or holding me back?

If your account is growing steadily—even if it dips occasionally—you're probably doing just fine.

Final Word: Stack Wins Over Time

Your performance doesn't have to be perfect—it just has to be consistent. One loss doesn't define you, and neither does one market dip. What matters is your record over time.

So keep contributing. Keep tracking. Keep learning. Because just like in your sport, the goal isn't to win every play—it's to finish the season strong.

And when it comes to money, the season is your life. Play it smart, play it long, and stack those financial wins.

Fees = Sneaky Turnovers

In sports, turnovers kill momentum. You could be driving down the field, dominating possession, or pulling away with a lead—but then, boom: a fumble, a bad pass, or a steal gives the ball to the other team. And just like that, you're backpedaling.

Investment fees are the sneaky turnovers of your financial game.

They might seem small, but over time, they can quietly rob you of serious money—and just like turnovers, they often happen when you're not paying attention.

What Are Investment Fees?

Fees are the costs you pay to manage or access your investments. Some are obvious, others are buried deep in fine print. Either way, they come straight out of your earnings—reducing how much money stays in your pocket.

Common types of investment fees include:

- Expense Ratios: This is the annual fee charged by mutual funds and ETFs to manage your money. It's shown as a percentage (like 0.03% or 1.25%).
- Account Maintenance Fees: Some platforms charge you just for having an account.
- Trading Fees: These are costs for buying or selling certain stocks or funds.
- Advisory Fees: If you work with a financial advisor, they might charge a flat rate or a percentage of your assets (often 1%).
-
- Hidden Fees: Some apps or funds might sneak in charges for "management" or "transactional services" that aren't super clear.

Even a small-sounding fee—like 1%—can cost you tens of thousands over time.

Turnover Example: 1% Fee Over Time

Let's say you invest $200 a month from age 22 to 50, earning an average return of 8% a year:

- With no fees, you'd have around $300,000 by age 50.
- With a 1% annual fee, your account could shrink to about $240,000.

That's a $60,000 turnover—just from fees.

You didn't lose the money in the market. You gave it up quietly every year... because you didn't realize the fee was eating away at your progress.

How to Avoid Fee Fumbles

1. Choose Low-Cost Index Funds or ETFs
2. Look for funds with expense ratios below 0.10% (Vanguard and Fidelity have some great options).
3. Use Fee-Free Platforms
4. Many brokers—like Schwab, Fidelity, and SoFi—offer no minimums, no trading fees, and no account maintenance charges.
5. Read the Fine Print
6. Don't just click "I agree." Understand what the fund or platform charges and when.
7. Ask Your Advisor
8. If you're working with a financial advisor, ask:

- How do you get paid?
- Do you charge a flat fee or a percentage?
- Are there any hidden costs I should know about?
- Track Your "Net Performance"

9. Don't just look at gross returns. Ask yourself: "What did I actually make after fees?"

Final Word: Protect Every Possession

You wouldn't be okay with handing the ball to the other team five times a game—so don't give up your money without knowing where it's going.

Every dollar lost to fees is a dollar that's not growing for your future.

So read the playbook, avoid sneaky turnovers, and keep your money on offense—where it belongs.

Part 4: Playing the Long Game

You've trained, competed, and maybe even won championships. But now it's time to prepare for your most important opponent yet: the future.

In sports, the best athletes don't just play for today—they play for the season, the playoffs, and their legacy. In life, your financial game works the same way. Short-term moves might feel good in the moment, but real success comes from playing the long game.

Up until now, this book has walked you through the foundations—budgeting, credit, taxes, investing, and making smart choices with your NIL money. But this next section is about what happens after the deals, after the games, and after the jersey comes off.

Because the truth is, even if you make it to the pros, you won't play forever. And if you don't? Life still goes on. And so do your bills, responsibilities, and opportunities to build wealth.

So what does it mean to play the long game financially?

It means you:

- Make decisions today that benefit your future self
- Think past your next NIL deal and plan for what's next
- Build relationships, not just brand deals

- Use money as a tool—not a trophy
- Protect yourself, your family, and your reputation

This section will help you:

- Plan for life after sports—whether that means going pro, starting a business, or pivoting into a new career
- Understand how to transition financially when NIL income stops
- Learn how to turn your experiences, brand, and audience into lasting opportunities
- Develop skills and habits that will serve you long after your athletic career ends
- Explore ways to support your family without sabotaging your financial future
- Build a professional network that opens doors far beyond sports
- Think bigger than NIL—think legacy

You'll also learn how to:

- Avoid the "shiny ball" syndrome—chasing quick wins and hype purchases
- Navigate big life moments like moving, marriage, having kids, or supporting loved ones
- Get serious about insurance, estate planning, and the kind of protection pros don't talk about enough

And perhaps most importantly, this section reminds you that your value doesn't end when your career does. In fact, this is where it begins.

Your NIL earnings may be temporary—but the habits, investments, and relationships you build now can last a lifetime. This is your chance to set yourself apart from the crowd—not just as an athlete, but as a leader, entrepreneur, and financially savvy young adult who made smart decisions when it counted most.

Because the scoreboard might turn off one day—but your life keeps playing.

Final Word: Think Beyond the Moment

If Part 1 was your preseason camp...

Part 2 your regular season...

Part 3 your strength training and playbook...

Then Part 4 is the postseason strategy that creates champions.

This is about legacy, leadership, and long-term wins.

Because the greatest athletes don't just dominate the game.

They master what comes after it.

Chapter 8: Insurance: Your Helmet

Let's be honest—insurance isn't the flashiest topic. It doesn't come with a sponsorship, a signing bonus, or a trending hashtag. But when life hits you hard—and it will—insurance is your helmet.

You wouldn't step onto the field without head protection. Why? Because you know one unexpected hit could end your season—or your career. The same is true in real life. Insurance protects your finances the way a helmet protects your head.

It doesn't stop the hit from happening—but it *does* make sure you survive it.

What Is Insurance, Really?

Insurance is a way to protect yourself financially from unexpected events—like injuries, accidents, lawsuits, or even the worst-case scenarios. You pay a small amount every month (called a premium) so that if something major happens, the insurance company helps cover the cost.

It's like having a teammate who steps in when the game goes sideways.

Types of Insurance Student-Athletes Should Know

1. Health Insurance

If you get hurt, health insurance covers hospital visits, surgeries, medications, and rehab. Some schools offer coverage—but it's not always complete.

Questions to ask your university:

- Does my athletic department cover all injuries?
- Do I need my own supplemental health plan?

2. Disability Insurance

If an injury keeps you from playing or stops your NIL opportunities, disability insurance can replace some of that lost income. This is especially important if you're earning a lot through brand deals.

Key point: If your school isn't paying for it, you may want to look into getting your own plan—especially if your NIL income is substantial.

3. Liability Insurance

What if you're doing a paid appearance and someone gets hurt or a brand accuses you of breaking a contract? Liability insurance protects you from being sued or held financially responsible.

4. Renters Insurance

If your apartment gets robbed or your laptop gets stolen, renters insurance covers the loss. It's cheap—usually $10–$20/month—but worth every penny if something goes wrong.

5. Life Insurance

Not always needed right away, but if you're supporting family or have dependents (like a child), life insurance ensures they're taken care of if something happens to you.

Why It Matters for NIL Athletes

Your NIL earnings make you a small business. That means you're exposed to more risks—and need more protection.

Imagine missing a whole season due to injury. Or losing thousands in gear during a break-in. Or having a deal canceled because of something outside your control. These things happen. And if you're not insured, you're the one stuck with the bill.

Final Word: Gear Up

You wouldn't play a full-contact sport without a helmet. Don't play the financial game without insurance.

It may not be fun, but it's foundational. It keeps you in the game when life throws a blindside hit.

Protect your money. Protect your future. Put your helmet on.

Analogy: Just Like You Wouldn't Step on the Field Without Pads, Don't Manage Money Without Protection

You wouldn't walk onto the field without your pads, would you? No shoulder pads, no helmet, no mouthguard—just you, raw and exposed, going full speed into contact? That's how careers end early. It's not just dangerous—it's reckless.

Managing your money without insurance is the same kind of risk.

In the financial world, your "pads" are insurance policies. They may not score touchdowns or show up in highlight reels, but when life hits hard—and it will—they absorb the impact. They keep you protected, standing, and moving forward.

So ask yourself: You train your body, protect your game, and guard your brand… why wouldn't you do the same for your money?

Pads = Protection = Peace of Mind

Let's break this down.

In football:

- Helmet = Head protection
- Shoulder pads = Absorb hits
- Mouthguard = Protect your jaw and teeth

In your financial life:

- Health Insurance = Protects your body and bank account from medical bills
- Disability Insurance = Protects your income if you can't work or perform
- Liability Insurance = Shields you from legal hits (like a lawsuit)
- Renters Insurance = Covers your stuff if it's stolen or damaged
- Life Insurance = Provides security for your family if something happens to you

Each one plays a role. Just like pads in a game, you hope you don't need them—but if you do, you'll be glad they're in place.

Why Student-Athletes Especially Need Protection

If you're earning money through NIL, you're more than just a player—you're now a personal brand and business.

That means:

- You may owe taxes
- You may travel, sign contracts, and handle gear or equipment
- You may face more risk (on the field *and* off)

Without insurance, one injury, accident, or legal issue can wipe out everything you've built.

It's not about living scared—it's about living smart. You don't skip the weight room because it's boring. You go because it prepares you for the big hits. Insurance works the same way.

Pro Tip: Ask the Right Questions

Just like you study film to prepare, study your financial playbook:

- Does your university cover injuries during competition *and* during NIL appearances?
- Are you insured if your NIL income stops because of injury?
- Do you have protection for your apartment, gear, laptop, or phone?
- If you're helping family financially, do you have a backup plan in case something happens?

Final Word: Suit Up

Managing your money without insurance is like playing linebacker with no helmet. It might work for a few plays... until it doesn't.

Insurance isn't exciting—but it's essential. It gives you security, peace of mind, and the ability to take smart risks knowing your downside is protected.

Because real pros don't just play hard—they play prepared.

Suit up your finances the same way you suit up for game day.

Disability Insurance: What If an Injury Ends Your Career?

It's every athlete's nightmare—you go up for a routine play, plant wrong, and boom. One snap, one twist, one hit, and suddenly everything changes.

Not just your season.

Not just your scholarship.

But your entire future.

You've probably thought about it physically: "Will I play again?" But what about financially?

If an injury ends your athletic career—what happens to your income, your NIL deals, your ability to earn through your name, image, and likeness?

That's where disability insurance comes in. It's the safety net no one talks about, but every athlete needs to understand.

What Is Disability Insurance?

Disability insurance replaces a portion of your income if you become unable to work due to an injury or illness. For student-athletes, that income might come from NIL endorsements, social media deals, or brand appearances.

If a serious injury takes you out of your sport—or even off social platforms—disability insurance can help you keep some money coming in. It won't replace your entire paycheck, but it can help you:

- Pay for school or living expenses
- Support family members
- Avoid going into debt

Stay financially stable while you recover or pivot

Why You Might Need It

Let's say you're earning $25,000 per year in NIL deals. Not bad for a college student. But all of that income depends on one thing: your ability to perform, show up, and represent your brand.

Now imagine a major injury—ACL tear, spinal issue, or even a concussion—that sidelines you for the season or ends your athletic future altogether.

Those NIL deals? They're likely gone.

That fan engagement on social? It might drop.

Your physical ability to represent a brand? Limited.

Disability insurance steps in when everything else steps out.

Who Pays for It?

Ask your school. Some universities provide disability insurance for athletes—especially if you're a top performer or expected to go pro.

Questions to ask your coach, compliance officer, or athletic department:

- Do we have disability insurance coverage through the school?
- Does it cover NIL-related income?
- Is there an option to get additional coverage on my own?

If your school doesn't provide it—or if your NIL income is significant—it may be smart to purchase private disability insurance. It's not cheap, but it can be customized to fit your unique situation.

Real Talk: Most Athletes Don't Think About This Until It's Too Late

You train hard, stay locked in, and assume everything will go as planned. But sports are unpredictable. Careers end early every year—not because of talent, but because of injury.

Disability insurance won't change the fact that you got hurt—but it can protect your finances while you recover and figure out your next move.

Final Word: Plan for the "What If"

You wear pads to protect your body.

You study film to protect your performance.

Disability insurance protects your financial future.

You hope you'll never need it—but if you do, you'll be glad you had it.

Because smart athletes protect their income as much as they protect their game.

Ask Your University: Do You Provide NIL or Injury Coverage?

When it comes to your future—don't assume, ask.

Just like you wouldn't walk into a game without knowing the game plan, you shouldn't go through your college career without knowing what kind of protection and support your school actually offers you.

As NIL opportunities grow, so do the risks. And while some schools have stepped up to provide resources, not all coverage is created equal.

Here are the key questions every student-athlete earning NIL income should ask their school:

1. Do You Provide NIL Insurance Coverage?

NIL income makes you a business. And like any business, you carry risk. Some universities now offer insurance options or resources to protect student-athletes' NIL earnings if something unexpected happens.

Ask:

- Is NIL-specific insurance available to me through the university?
- If not, is there a provider or program you recommend?
- Does the school offer group rates for private policies?

2. Do You Provide Injury (Disability) Insurance?

This is a big one. Your athletic ability is tied to your income, your opportunities, and your brand. If an injury ends your career—or sidelines you for a long time—disability insurance can step in to replace part of your lost income.

Ask:

- Do you provide disability insurance for student-athletes?
- Does it cover both athletic performance *and* NIL income?
- If not, can I purchase my own plan and still maintain eligibility?

3. Who Pays for the Insurance?

Even if coverage is available, make sure you understand who's footing the bill.

Ask:

- Is this something the athletic department pays for?
- Am I responsible for paying premiums out of pocket?
- Are there scholarships or grants that cover this kind of protection?

4. What Happens If I Get Injured During a NIL Activity (Not Team-Related)?

Say you get hurt doing a photo shoot or attending an event for a brand deal. That's not a team practice—but it's still part of your income. Who's responsible for your care and financial protection?

Ask:

- Am I still covered under the school's policy if the injury happens during a NIL-related appearance?
- Will that impact my scholarship or eligibility?

Final Word: Get Clarity Now, Not Regret Later

Too many student-athletes assume they're protected—until something happens. Don't wait for a crisis to find out what your coverage actually includes.

Ask questions. Take notes. Loop in your compliance officer or athletic trainer.

Because in this new era of college sports, protecting your body and your brand is part of your job—and you have the right to know who has your back.

Health, Liability, and NIL-Specific Insurance Matter

You already protect your body with gear, your game with film study, and your future with discipline. But in the new world of NIL, there are three critical types of insurance you need to understand if you want to protect your *brand, bank account,* and *well-being*:

Health insurance, liability insurance, and NIL-specific insurance.

Each one plays a unique role in your off-field defense, and together they form your personal protection plan. You wouldn't play a game without coverage—don't run your business without it either.

1. Health Insurance: The Non-Negotiable

You know how quickly things can change on the field. One awkward landing, one wrong step, and you could be facing surgery, physical therapy, and a stack of medical bills.

Health insurance covers:

- Doctor and hospital visits
- Surgeries and rehabilitation
- Medications and follow-up care

Why it matters:

Whether you're covered by your parents, your university, or a private plan, you must have health insurance—especially if you're traveling, attending brand events, or doing NIL work off campus.

Ask your school:

- What does the athletic department cover?
- Does that coverage extend to NIL-related injuries?
- Do I need additional health insurance if I'm doing NIL appearances on my own?

2. Liability Insurance: Protection From the Unexpected

Let's say you're doing a paid appearance at a camp and a participant gets injured. Or you post something on social media and a brand claims it harmed their reputation. Or you accidentally damage equipment during a photo shoot. These things happen—and when they do, you could be legally and financially responsible.

Liability insurance protects you from lawsuits, claims, and financial loss.

Why it matters:

You're now a public figure and a brand. That means you carry more legal risk than the average college student. Liability coverage gives you peace of mind in case something unexpected happens.

Ask your advisor or insurance agent:

- Can I get personal liability coverage for my NIL business?
- Does my renters or auto policy include any liability protection?
- Are there NIL-specific policies that include this coverage?

3. NIL-Specific Insurance: For Your Personal Brand

NIL-specific insurance is designed for student-athletes earning money through sponsorships, endorsements, or appearances. It helps protect:

- Lost NIL income due to injury or illness
- Legal fees related to contract disputes
- Reputation management services (in some cases)

Why it matters:

If your NIL income stops because of something beyond your control—like an injury or eligibility issue—NIL-specific insurance can help fill the financial gap.

Ask your university and agent:

- Do you offer or recommend NIL-specific coverage?
- What does it protect, and what are the limits?
- Are group plans available for student-athletes?

Final Word: Don't Just Play the Game—Protect It

You've worked too hard to leave your future exposed.

Health, liability, and NIL-specific insurance aren't optional—they're essential.

They won't make you go viral. They won't get likes. But they will keep you in the game when life throws a flag.

Suit up, protect your assets, and play smart.

Chapter 9: Networking & Alumni Your Teammates for Life

When you leave the locker room for the last time, the scoreboard goes dark—but the game of life is just getting started.

And one of the most powerful assets you can take with you isn't a trophy or a stat line—it's your network.

Networking is your off-the-field team.

It's made up of people—coaches, professors, alumni, former teammates, brand reps, professionals—who can help guide, connect, and open doors for you long after your playing days are over.

Just like you rely on teammates to execute a play, win games, or push you in practice, you'll rely on your network to help you win at life.

Why Networking Matters for Student-Athletes

As a student-athlete, you're in a unique position. People respect your work ethic, your time management, your discipline, and your ability to perform under pressure. But once your playing days end, it's your relationships—not your stat sheet—that will move you forward.

Here's what a strong network can help you do:

- Land internships and job offers
- Launch a business or get clients
- Get introduced to mentors or investors

- Find speaking gigs or media opportunities
- Learn about industries you might want to enter

Athletic talent may open the first door—but connections are what keep doors opening.

Start with Your Alumni Network

Your school's alumni base is full of former athletes, entrepreneurs, doctors, lawyers, CEOs, and people in every field imaginable. And guess what? Many of them *want* to help you—especially if they were once in your cleats.

Tips to tap into your alumni network:

- Attend alumni events, even virtually
- Introduce yourself after games or speaking engagements
- Ask your coaches, professors, or athletic department for intros
- Use LinkedIn to connect with alumni in your desired career field

Don't be afraid to reach out. Say something simple like:

"Hey [Name], I'm a current student-athlete at [School], and I'd love to hear about your career journey. Do you have 15 minutes for a quick Zoom or call?"

That one message could change your life.

Relationships Over Résumés

You don't need a 4.0 or the perfect résumé to start building relationships. Be real. Be respectful. Be curious.

Networking isn't about asking for a job—it's about building genuine connections, learning from others, and staying top of mind when opportunities arise.

It's not just what you know, or even who you know—it's who knows you.

Final Word: Build Your Off-the-Field Team

Your college teammates may not be with you forever, but your network can last a lifetime.

Invest in your relationships like you invest in your game.

Show up. Stay connected. Give value when you can. And when it's time to transition—from student-athlete to professional—you won't be doing it alone.

Because in the game of life, your best teammates might not wear jerseys anymore—but they've still got your back.

Analogy: A Great Network Is Like a Great Locker Room – It Makes You Better

Think about the best locker rooms you've ever been in.

The ones where everyone held each other accountable.

Where there was laughter, support, and shared goals.

Where people pushed you to be your best—on and off the field.

That kind of environment doesn't just help you win games—it helps you grow.

Now take that energy off the field. That's what a great network feels like.

A great network is like a great locker room—it makes you better. It's filled with people who challenge you, encourage you, guide you, and genuinely want to see you succeed.

Your Locker Room Didn't Just Happen—You Built It

You didn't just magically end up with a group of teammates who made you better. You practiced together, went through hard times together, won and lost together. You invested in those relationships. And the reward? A support system.

Your professional network works the same way.

It's not just about collecting contacts—it's about building real connections.

The people in your network might:

- Help you get your first internship
- Introduce you to a mentor in your dream field
- Recommend you for a job or opportunity
- Share insights from industries you're curious about
- Offer life advice when you're going through a transition

But they can't do any of that if they don't know who you are.

Create a Locker Room Around Your Future

Start now—while you're still on campus.

Build relationships with:

- Professors who see your discipline
- Alumni who once wore your jersey
- Brand reps you've worked with through NIL
- Coaches and support staff
- Students outside of athletics with different skill sets

Stay in touch. Check in. Offer to help when you can. And always follow up with gratitude and intention.

Because just like in sports, the locker room culture you build off the field will impact the level you play at for the rest of your life.

The Best Networks Are Built on Trust

Remember how you earned your teammates' trust? By showing up, putting in the work, staying humble, and leading when it mattered.

That same formula builds strong professional relationships.

Don't be the person who only shows up when they need something. Be the one who:

- Asks questions
- Listens well
- Follows through
- Lifts others up

People don't forget that kind of energy.

Final Word: Choose the Right Locker Room for Your Life

Surround yourself with people who challenge you to think bigger.

People who've already been where you want to go.

People who don't let you settle for potential—they push you to produce.

Because just like in sports, the right locker room makes average players great—and great players legendary.

In life, your network *is* your locker room. So fill it with teammates who make you better.

How to Connect with Alumni, Mentors, and Future Business Partners

In your sport, success comes from relationships—between teammates, coaches, and the community around you. The same is true in your career. Whether you want to launch a business, work in sports media, join a nonprofit, or become an entrepreneur, who you know can shape where you go.

And here's the good news: as a student-athlete, you already have a powerful network waiting for you—alumni, former athletes, local business leaders, and professionals who respect your discipline and drive.

The key? You just have to reach out and build those connections. Here's how:

1. Start with Alumni—They're Already on Your Team

Alumni love helping athletes who came through the same program or school they did. Many of them were in your shoes not too long ago.

How to connect:

- Use LinkedIn: Search your school's alumni page. Filter by industry or city. Look for "former student-athlete" in their bio.
- Send a message like:
- "Hi [Name], I'm a student-athlete at [University], and I noticed you're working in [field]. I'd love to learn about your career path and any advice you might have for someone just getting started."
-
- Show up: Attend alumni mixers, homecoming events, or any speaker panels where you can meet grads face-to-face.

Pro tip: Always follow up with a thank-you message and keep the relationship alive with an occasional check-in.

2. Find a Mentor—Someone 5–10 Years Ahead of You

A mentor is someone who's walked the path you're trying to take—someone who can help you avoid mistakes, see opportunities, and grow both professionally and personally.

Where to look:

- Professors who support athletes
- Coaches and staff in the athletic department
- Former teammates who've moved on to careers you admire
- Professionals you meet through NIL deals or internships

How to approach:

- Be direct but respectful. Say:
- "I admire the work you're doing in [industry], and I'm trying to learn more. Would you be open to connecting once a month or so to talk about your journey and answer a few questions?"

Most people are flattered to be asked. And if they say yes? Show up on time, ask good questions, and listen more than you speak.

3. Build Relationships with Future Business Partners Now

If you plan to start a business—or just want to collaborate with driven people—start identifying peers who are creative, ambitious, and smart. These might be:

- Classmates in your major
- Teammates who are into content creation or finance
- Student entrepreneurs on campus

How to connect:

- Work on a class project together
- Attend entrepreneurship events or NIL summits
- Pitch an idea over coffee or a casual Zoom chat

Remember: some of the most successful business teams in the world started with two college students talking about ideas in a dorm room.

Final Word: Relationships > Résumés

You don't need a perfect résumé to build a powerful network.

You just need to show up, be real, and follow through.

Start now. Stay curious. Build your team off the field—because they'll help you win long after the season ends.

Don't Just Chase Fans—Build Relationships

Social media has changed the game. With NIL, your followers can help you land deals, build a brand, and expand your reach. But here's the truth no one tells you:

Followers aren't the same as relationships.

A large following might get you attention—but meaningful connections are what create long-term opportunities. Fans cheer for you. Relationships invest in you.

That means if you want your brand and business to grow after the cheers fade, you can't just focus on likes and clout. You need to focus on people who will walk with you, not just watch you.

Why Relationships Matter More Than Followers

In the NIL space, it's tempting to chase quick wins:

- Viral posts
- One-time checks
- Surface-level deals with trendy brands

But if you want a career that lasts—on or off the field—you need depth, not just reach.

Brand reps, alumni, mentors, and even fans are far more likely to support you long-term if they know who you are beyond your jersey.

And that only happens through real connection.

The Difference Between Fans and Relationships

Fans

Relationships

Clap for your wins (Fans)

Ask how you're really doing **(Relationships)**

Follow your highlight reel (Fans)

Stick around through tough moments **(Relationships)**

Might buy your merch (Fans)

Might offer you a job or opportunity **(Relationships)**

Celebrate your game days (Fans)

Help shape your post-game future **(Relationships)**

Having a million followers is great. But having 10 strong professional relationships can lead to:

- Internships
- Business partnerships
- Career mentorship
- Investment opportunities
- Life-changing guidance

Followers know your name. Relationships know your story.

How to Build Real Relationships in the NIL Era

1. Engage Beyond the Comments
2. Don't just say "thanks!" on your posts. Send DMs to supporters, ask questions, and find ways to connect beyond the platform.
3. Be Interested, Not Just Interesting
4. Ask about other people's work, interests, and goals. Listen more than you talk. That's how trust is built.
5. Follow Up and Follow Through
6. Had a great conversation with an alum or brand rep? Don't ghost them.

Send a quick thank-you message or follow up with an update.

7. Be Consistent in Who You Are
8. People support athletes they can trust. Be authentic, respectful, and honest in all your communication—online and in person.

Final Word: Build a Team Off the Field

Your fans may pack the stands, but it's your relationships that will help carry you after the buzzer sounds.

Don't just chase clout—cultivate connection.

Don't just aim to impress—aim to build.

Because popularity fades. Followers come and go.

But the right relationships?

They'll walk with you long after the lights go out.

Chapter 10: Entrepreneurship & Real Estate Building Wealth Beyond the Game

You've spent your whole life learning how to compete, lead, and perform under pressure. You've built discipline, time management, and communication skills most people don't develop until much later.

That's why entrepreneurship and real estate are natural next steps for many athletes.

These paths let you take the same mindset you've used in sports—and apply it to business and ownership. Whether you're launching a brand, starting a company, or buying your first property, these moves can help you turn temporary NIL income into long-term wealth.

Let's explore both.

Entrepreneurship: Turning NIL Into a Business

Entrepreneurship isn't just about having an idea. It's about building something that solves a problem or adds value—and getting paid for it.

As a student-athlete, your NIL earnings can help fund:

- A clothing or lifestyle brand
- A training/coaching business
- A media platform or podcast
- A digital product or online course

- A nonprofit that supports your community

The possibilities are endless—but the key is thinking long-term.

Use your NIL to:

- Cover startup costs (website, logo, gear, software)
- Pay for mentorship, courses, or coaching
- Hire help (designers, editors, business advisors)
- Promote your business on social media while your platform is hot

Pro tip: If you're starting a business, consider creating an LLC or S-Corp. It can offer legal protection, make taxes easier, and make you look more professional to sponsors and investors.

Real Estate: Owning Assets, Not Just Renting Space

Buying property is one of the most time-tested ways to build wealth. If you handle your finances wisely, real estate can help you turn NIL income into something that grows even after the deals stop.

You don't need to wait until you're rich. Student-athletes are already investing in:

- Rental properties in their college town
- Short-term rentals like Airbnb
- House hacking—buying a small property, living in one room, and renting out the others

Why real estate matters:

- Your property can grow in value (appreciation)
- You can generate steady monthly income (cash flow)
- It can provide tax benefits (depreciation, deductions)

NIL Tip: Use your NIL income as part of a down payment or to improve your credit score so you can qualify for a loan. Talk to a real estate-savvy financial advisor who can help you run the numbers before jumping in.

Final Word: Be the Boss, Own the Building

Whether you're running your own business or collecting rent from tenants, entrepreneurship and real estate give you control.

They help you move from earning a check to cutting your own.

From renting a space to owning the block.

So while NIL gives you a chance to make money *today*, these two paths help you build freedom for tomorrow.

Because in the game of life, real wealth isn't just about how much you make—it's about how much you own.

Use NIL to Seed Your Future Business

You've probably heard the saying, *"Use the money you earn today to fund the life you want tomorrow."*

That's exactly what your NIL income can do for you.

Right now, NIL deals may feel like extra cash—something to spend, flex, or enjoy. And yes, you should enjoy some of it. But if you're thinking like a future entrepreneur, you'll realize this: NIL is your seed money. It's startup capital. It's the money most people have to borrow to build their first business—but you're earning it in college.

Smart athletes use NIL to plant the seeds for something bigger.

Why NIL Is the Perfect Launchpad

Most college students don't have the luxury of starting a business with real capital. They're in debt, working part-time, and scraping together funds to make things happen.

You? You're already earning. And you've got:

- A platform
- A built-in audience
- A personal brand
- Real income

That's exactly what entrepreneurs dream of. The only difference between you and a startup founder is focus and execution.

Business Ideas You Can Start with NIL Capital

Not sure what to build? Here are business ideas that pair well with your personal brand and NIL experience:

- Fitness & Coaching: Offer training plans, online classes, or a personal coaching service
- Apparel or Lifestyle Brand: Launch your own logo, slogan, or athlete-inspired merch line
- Content Creation Agency: Use your social media skills to help other athletes build their brand
- Podcast or YouTube Channel: Build a platform where you interview athletes, coaches, or influencers
- Community Initiatives: Start a nonprofit or foundation tied to something you care about

You don't need to know everything. Start small, invest a little, learn as you go. Use NIL earnings to cover:

- Website costs
- Logo and branding
- Business licenses or LLC setup
- Inventory or equipment
- Marketing and social media promotion
- Mentorship, coaching, or courses to level up your skills

Think Like a Business Owner Now

Using NIL to seed a business means shifting your mindset from spending to investing.

It's asking yourself:

- "What will this money build for me?"
- "How can I use this income to create more income?"
- "What do I want my name and legacy to stand for beyond sports?"

You're already the CEO of your brand—why not be the CEO of a business too?

Final Word: Don't Just Take the Check—Flip It

NIL is a blessing. But it's temporary.

Your business? That can last a lifetime.

So don't just take every check and spend it like it's gone tomorrow.

Use some of that money to plant roots—create something that will grow even when your playing career is over.

Seed your business now. Own your future later. That's the real NIL play.

Should You Form an LLC? (Spoiler: Maybe)

Once you start earning real money through NIL, it's not just side cash anymore—it's a business. And like any business, you might be wondering:

"Should I form an LLC?"

Short answer?

Maybe.

It depends on how much you're making, what you're doing, and how serious you are about building a long-term brand or business.

Let's break it down so you can make the call.

What Is an LLC?

LLC stands for Limited Liability Company. It's a legal structure that separates *you* from your business. It's one of the easiest and most popular ways to start a business—especially for freelancers, creators, and entrepreneurs (a.k.a. NIL athletes).

Forming an LLC means your NIL work becomes its own business entity. Instead of being "You, the person," you're now "You, the company."

Benefits of Having an LLC

1. Legal Protection
2. If something goes wrong—like a contract dispute, someone tries to sue, or a brand claims you didn't deliver—your personal assets are protected. That means your bank account, car, and personal stuff aren't on the line
3. Professional Credibility
4. Brands, sponsors, and businesses may take you more seriously when you're operating under a real business name. Having "LLC" next to your brand can elevate how you're seen in negotiations and contracts.
5. Easier Business Banking & Contracts
6. You can open a business bank account, which makes it easier to track income, pay expenses, and keep your taxes organized. Also, some brands may prefer to pay a business, not an individual.
7. Tax Flexibility

As an LLC, you can still file taxes as an individual (sole proprietor), or you can elect to be taxed as an S-Corp if it benefits you. You may also unlock business deductions—expenses you can subtract from your income to lower your tax bill (think website fees, gear, travel, marketing, etc.).

Reasons to Wait on an LLC

- You're making under $5,000/year in NIL income
- You're still figuring out your brand and don't have consistent deals
- You haven't done much beyond social media posting and one-time partnerships
- You're not ready to keep up with business records, taxes, and paperwork

That's okay. You can still track your income, save for taxes, and act professionally without an LLC. But as your earnings grow—or your business goals get bigger—you'll want that structure in place.

What's Involved in Forming an LLC?

- Filing with your state (usually $50–$300)
- Picking a business name
- Choosing a registered agent (can be you or a service)
- Opening a business bank account
- Keeping track of your income and expenses
-

You can do it yourself online, or hire a service like LegalZoom, ZenBusiness, or even ask your CPA for help.

Final Word: If NIL Is a Side Hustle, Maybe Not. If It's a Business, Probably Yes.

Forming an LLC isn't required—but it can level up your brand, protect your money, and position you for bigger opportunities.

So if NIL is becoming more than a moment, treat it like a movement—and maybe make it official.

Buying vs. Renting — Smart Moves for Stability

Whether you're on campus or thinking ahead to life after graduation, housing is one of the biggest expenses—and decisions—you'll face. The question is: Should you rent or buy?

It depends on your goals, your financial situation, and how long you plan to stay in one place. Both options have pros and cons, but what matters most is making a smart move that sets you up for stability.

Let's break it down.

Renting: Flexibility Over Ownership

Renting is usually the go-to option for college students and young adults, and for good reason—it's simple and flexible.

Pros of Renting:

- Low upfront cost: You usually just need first month's rent and a security deposit
- No maintenance responsibilities: If something breaks, it's the landlord's job to fix it
- Flexibility: You can move after your lease ends, perfect if you're not sure where you'll be in a year
- Short-term commitment: No long-term debt or mortgage

Cons of Renting:

- No equity: You're paying to live there, but you don't own anything
- Rent can increase: Landlords can raise rent when your lease renews
- Limited control: You can't make big changes, and you're subject to rules (no pets, no painting, etc.)

When renting makes sense:

- You're in college or just graduated
- You don't know where you'll be living next year
- You're not ready for the responsibilities of owning a home
- You want to save more before committing

Buying: Ownership and Long-Term Wealth

Buying a home means you're building something—equity. Every mortgage payment gets you closer to owning the property outright, and real estate often grows in value over time.

Pros of Buying:

- You build equity: Your monthly payments go toward ownership, not a landlord
- Property may increase in value: If the home goes up in value, you can profit when you sell
- Stable monthly payments: If you get a fixed-rate mortgage, your payment won't change
- You're the boss: Paint the walls, add a gym, rent out a room—it's your call

Cons of Buying:

- Big upfront costs: Down payment, closing costs, inspections, etc.

- Maintenance is on you: Roof leaks? You pay to fix it
- Less flexibility: Selling a home takes time, and you could lose money if you sell too soon
- Credit and debt matter: You'll need a good credit score and proof of income to qualify for a mortgage

When buying makes sense:

- You're financially stable with a steady income (maybe from NIL)
- You plan to stay in the area for 3+ years
- You have money saved for a down payment
- You're ready for responsibility and see real estate as part of your wealth plan

Final Word: Live Smart Now, Own Smart Later

You don't have to buy right now to make smart moves.

Start by building credit, saving, and learning. Use your NIL income to prepare for future opportunities—maybe that's a rental property, maybe it's your first home.

Renting gives you freedom now. Buying gives you stability later. Either way, being intentional with where you live sets the foundation for financial peace.

Play the long game—on the field and with your address.

Keep Good Records: It's Your Game Film for the IRS

You wouldn't play in a championship game without studying film.

Film proves how hard you worked. It shows what you did right, what needs improvement, and how you stack up against the competition. It backs up your performance.

That's exactly what financial records are for—but instead of your coach reviewing them, it's the IRS.

Once you start earning NIL income, you're a business. And just like any business, you're expected to keep receipts, track income, and be able to back up what you put on your tax return.

No records? No defense.

And when the IRS starts asking questions, not having proof can cost you—big time.

Why You Need to Track Everything

As a student-athlete with NIL deals, you're responsible for accurately reporting how much money you made, what you spent to run your business, and what taxes you owe. If you don't have good records, you could:

- Miss out on tax deductions that lower your bill
- Pay more than you actually owe
- Face penalties or interest
- Struggle through a tax audit without proper documentation

Good recordkeeping isn't about being paranoid—it's about being prepared. It also makes you a more focused and professional entrepreneur.

What You Should Be Keeping Track Of

Income

Track every dollar you make through NIL—sponsorships, partnerships, speaking gigs, social media posts, merch sales, and appearances. Whether it's $50 or $5,000, write it down. Use a spreadsheet, a notes app, or an online tool like QuickBooks or Wave to log every payment.

Expenses

Keep track of anything you pay for that supports your NIL brand or business. This might include:

- Travel (gas, flights, hotels for appearances or shoots)

- Gear (camera equipment, lighting, uniforms)
- Digital tools (apps, website hosting, editing software)
- Marketing (designers, video editors, ad spend)
- Legal and business support (contract review, consultations)

Receipts and Invoices

Every purchase related to your brand? Save the receipt. If you hire someone—like a graphic designer or photographer—ask for an invoice. You may need this proof if the IRS ever asks you to explain your tax deductions.

Contracts

Save every NIL deal you sign. Keep both digital and printed copies, labeled by company and date. These contracts confirm how much you agreed to be paid and what you were responsible for doing.

Tax Forms

In January, companies that paid you over $600 will send you a 1099-NEC form. These forms also go to the IRS, so you need to include them in your tax return. Hold on to all tax documents in a safe place.

Make It a Habit

Pick one day a week to update your records. It only takes 10–15 minutes to review your income, add any receipts, and save new contracts. Just like film study, the more consistent you are, the smoother things go when it counts.

Final Word: Preparation Beats Pressure

Good records are your protection.

They prove you're handling your NIL business like a pro.

They save you money, time, and stress.

Treat them like game film—study them, use them, and never go into tax season without them.

Chapter 11: When the Game Ends

Every athlete hears it at some point, whether they're ready or not:

"The game doesn't last forever."

It's not a threat—it's a truth. Your body won't always perform the way it does now. The stadium lights eventually shut off. The final whistle blows. And whether that's after college, a short pro career, or never going pro at all, one thing is guaranteed:

The game will end.

But here's the part no one tells you:

What you do now will shape what happens next.

Are You Ready for Life After Sports?

Too many athletes are surprised when it's over. They've built their identity around being an athlete, and when that chapter closes, they don't know who they are without the game.

But you're more than a number on a jersey.

You're disciplined, competitive, coachable, focused. Those qualities don't disappear when you hang up your cleats—they transfer.

The question is: Have you built anything else while you've been playing?

- Have you saved any of your NIL money?
- Have you built relationships outside of sports?
- Have you started investing in your future self?
- Do you have a plan for what's next?

Even a Little Saved Now Grows Into a Lot Later

Let's talk numbers.

If you take just $250/month from your NIL income and invest it consistently starting in college, by age 50, you could have over $400,000 thanks to compound interest. That's not a dream—that's math.

But if you spend it all trying to keep up with the "lifestyle" of being an athlete—new shoes, trips, jewelry, expensive cars—you might end up with memories and receipts… but nothing that grows.

The game might end, but your money can keep playing—if you play it right.

This Is Your Window

College is one of the few times you're surrounded by:

- Free resources (advisors, alumni, mentors)
- A large support network
- A personal brand at its peak

Use this time to:

- Build your financial habits
- Learn how to manage income and taxes
- Create a brand that extends beyond sports
- Network with professionals and alumni
- Take internships or side projects in the offseason
- Invest in your future, even if it's just $50 at a time

Because when the game ends, you don't want to start from zero—you want to already be in motion.

Final Word: The Game Ends, But Life Keeps Going

You're not just an athlete—you're an entrepreneur, a leader, a future professional in whatever field you choose.

Use NIL wisely. Stack your wins now. Make decisions the future you will thank you for. Because one day, your sport will say goodbye.

Make sure you've built a life—and a legacy—that's just getting started.

Because when the game ends, your next chapter begins. And if you've played the long game right, it'll be your biggest win yet.

Life After Sports: Not a Loss, Just the Next Quarter

You've played your heart out for years. Early mornings. Long practices. Long bus rides. Big wins. Tough losses. You've poured everything into your sport. It's been your identity, your structure, your passion.

And then one day, it's over.

No more practices. No more film sessions. No more game-day butterflies. The cheering quiets. The routines stop. And suddenly, you're asking: *"Now what?"*

Let's get something clear right now:

Life after sports isn't a loss. It's just the next quarter.

The first quarter was about becoming an athlete.

This next one? It's about becoming the person who takes everything you learned on the field—and uses it to win at life.

The Skills You've Built Aren't Going Anywhere

You might not be suiting up anymore, but your habits, mindset, and discipline are still with you. In fact, they're your competitive edge off the field.

Think about it:

- Time management? You've mastered it.
- Accountability? You've lived it daily.
- Mental toughness? You've built it through injuries, setbacks, and pressure moments.
- Leadership? You've done it with teammates, coaches, and under the spotlight.

Now it's time to transfer those skills from the locker room to the boardroom, classroom, business world, or wherever your path leads.

Prepare for the Transition—Before the Buzzer Sounds

Some athletes wait until the game ends to figure out what's next. But the best ones—just like in sports—prepare before the final play.

While you're still in the game:

- Use your NIL income to start investing or saving
- Explore career paths through internships, networking, or shadowing
- Build relationships with alumni, faculty, and professionals
- Develop your personal brand beyond your sport
- Take time to reflect on what you're passionate about off the field

When you treat your time as an athlete like the first quarter of your life, you stop fearing the end. You start preparing for a strong second quarter—and beyond.

New Game, New Goals

Maybe your new goal is to start a business.

Maybe it's to give back to your community.

Maybe it's to lead, teach, coach, or inspire.

Whatever it is, you don't have to start over—you just have to keep going. The rules might change, but the effort, focus, and drive that made you a great athlete? That's your superpower in the real world.

Final Word: Halftime Is Just a Pause—Not the End

You didn't lose the game. You just finished a quarter.

Now's your chance to regroup, re-strategize, and come out of the tunnel with new goals, new purpose, and a new jersey—one that says entrepreneur, creator, coach, leader, or whatever title you choose.

Life after sports isn't the end of your story—it's the beginning of your next championship run.

So take a breath, square your shoulders, and get ready.

Because the next quarter is yours.

If You Save/Invest Smart Now, You'll Have Options Later

When you're in college, it can feel like life is coming at you fast—classes, practices, games, social life, NIL deals, maybe even a side hustle. Thinking about retirement or life in your 30s or 40s feels like trying to game-plan for a season that hasn't even started yet.

But here's the truth:

The smart money moves you make now don't just help you later—they give you freedom.

Not just the freedom to retire early (though that's nice), but freedom to choose your future.

Freedom to say "yes" to what matters and "no" to what doesn't.

Freedom to walk away from bad deals or bad jobs.

Freedom to take a risk on something you care about.

And that freedom starts with how you manage your money—right now.

Chapter 12: International Student-Athletes & NIL

Navigating the Rules, Risks, and Opportunities

If you're an international student-athlete, you're likely juggling more than most of your teammates. On top of school, sports, and NIL opportunities, you're also dealing with immigration status, visa restrictions, and unclear policies. While NIL has created new income streams for U.S.-based athletes, the playbook looks very different for international athletes.

This chapter is here to help you understand:

- What your visa allows (and doesn't allow)
- How to protect your eligibility and legal status
- What smart, safe NIL participation could look like for you
- And what resources can help you navigate it all

Your F-1 Visa and Why It Matters

Most international student-athletes in the U.S. are on an F-1 student visa. This visa is designed for full-time academic study—and it comes with strict rules about earning income in the U.S.

F-1 visa limits include:

- You cannot work off-campus unless it's approved by the government (like OPT or CPT).

- You cannot receive traditional NIL income while inside the U.S.—because it may be considered unauthorized employment.
- Violating these rules could put your visa—and your eligibility to stay in the country—at risk.

Bottom line:

You must talk to your school's international student office or Designated School Official (DSO) *before* signing any NIL deal. They are the gatekeepers for visa compliance.

What NIL Opportunities Might Be Allowed

Although in-country work is limited, there are creative, compliant ways international athletes can explore NIL opportunities:

1. Deals Outside the U.S.

You may be able to sign or fulfill NIL deals while you're physically outside of the United States (e.g., during breaks or summers at home).

2. Monetizing Your Brand at Home

If your country permits it, you can monetize your name, image, and likeness with international brands while back home—social media, endorsements, even hosting camps.

3. Creating Content Abroad

If you create, post, or deliver content while you're outside of the U.S., it's typically considered foreign-earned income.

4. Licensing or Trademarking Your Brand

You can build and protect your personal brand while in the U.S. (e.g., creating a logo, trademarking your name) without "working."

Legal and Financial Issues to Watch

1. Taxes

Even if you earn NIL income outside the U.S., you may still owe taxes in the U.S., your home country, or both. Use a CPA who specializes in international tax law.

2. Banking

Make sure your bank accounts are set up properly and legally. Some U.S. banks restrict certain types of transfers or foreign income reporting.

3. Contracts

Avoid signing any NIL contract without having it reviewed by a sports attorney and your school's compliance office. The wrong signature could cost you your visa.

4. Business Formation

Forming an LLC or business may raise red flags for visa holders. Never create a business in the U.S. without legal counsel.

Smart Moves for International Student-Athletes

- Track Everything: If you do any NIL work abroad, document dates, locations, contracts, and payments.
- Stay Informed: Rules are evolving. Follow updates from your athletic department, the NCAA, and your school's legal team.
- Build the Brand Now: You can still grow your social presence, build a media kit, and develop your skills even if you can't earn right away.
- Plan for the Future: Post-graduation opportunities like Optional Practical Training (OPT) or H-1B visas may open the door to NIL income legally.
- Use Summer Breaks Wisely: If you return home during the summer, that may be your best time to fulfill NIL deals, shoot content, or launch a brand legally.

Questions to Ask Your School

1. Am I allowed to participate in NIL activities under my visa?
2. What types of NIL activities are considered "work" under U.S. law?
3. Can I fulfill NIL obligations while outside the country?
4. Will my OPT or CPT eligibility be affected by NIL?
5. Can I be paid through a foreign bank or third-party business?

Final Word: Caution First, Opportunity Second

As an international athlete, you have every right to build your brand and plan for your future. But when it comes to NIL, your immigration status is non-negotiable. Don't risk your education, your eligibility, or your ability to stay in the U.S. just to make a quick dollar.

Play the long game. Build your network. Learn the system. And when the rules finally catch up to the reality of your talent, you'll be ready—with a brand that's global, strategic, and built to last.

Chapter 13: Culture: The Lens That Shapes How You See Money

Financial literacy doesn't begin with a budget or a bank account. It begins with your story. It begins with how you were raised, what you were exposed to, and the experiences — good or bad — that shaped your relationship with money.

Let's keep it real: depending on your race, gender, religion, upbringing, and environment, you're going to see money through a different lens than the person next to you. And that's okay. In fact, it's *essential* to understand this if you're going to build wealth that lasts.

Your Lens Is Unique

If you were raised by a single mom holding down multiple jobs just to put food on the table, where the only conversations about money were about not having enough of it, then *of course* your relationship with money is different. You may feel pressure to earn as much as possible, as fast as possible. You might struggle with guilt when spending or saving because scarcity was the norm.

If you grew up in a neighborhood where drug dealers drove the nicest cars and wore the nicest clothes — and sports was your only way out — then yeah, money might represent freedom, status, or even survival. That's your lens. Your hustle was born from survival. But now, it's time to pivot from *survival mode* to *wealth mode*.

If you found out, years later, that your uncle or someone close to you used your Social Security number and racked up thousands in debt before you were even 18 — then trust issues around money are valid. That betrayal can shape how much you trust banks, credit systems, and even professionals.

No matter what your background is — Black, white, brown, green — *it all comes down to exposure.* Exposure to knowledge. Exposure to what's possible. Exposure to the tools that weren't handed to you growing up.

You Can't Change Where You Come From — But You Can Change Where You're Going

The way forward starts with educating yourself, and this book is part of that journey. Don't let anyone — not your coach, your agent, your accountant, or even your teammate — tell you that financial literacy isn't for you. *You* are your first line of defense.

People will tell you "that's your financial advisor's job" or "your agent will take care of that." Nah. Make them teach you.

- If you have a financial advisor — ask them to break it down.
- If you're working with a CPA — understand your taxes.
- If you have an agent or a manager — demand transparency in your deals.

Every professional on your team works *for* you. But if you don't understand the playbook, how will you know if they're running the right plays?

Learn the Game — So You Don't Get Played

Every year, we see headlines about athletes — even pros — who get taken advantage of. Millions lost. Careers cut short. Financial ruin. The saddest part? In most cases, it wasn't because they didn't *make* enough money. It's because they didn't *understand* what was being done with it.

This is why culture matters. If you were taught to keep quiet, to trust the system, or to avoid talking about money altogether — *break that cycle.* Ask questions. Get uncomfortable. Demand answers.

Read this book. Read *other* books. Listen to podcasts. Watch YouTube videos. Take courses. You don't have to be a finance major to understand your own money. You just have to *care enough to learn.*

This Is Bigger Than You

Let's be real — you might be the first in your family to have a shot at real money. You might be the first to sign an NIL deal, to start a business, or to even think about generational wealth. That's not pressure — that's *power.*

Learn the game so you can teach it to your younger siblings, cousins, teammates, or even your future kids. Be the one who changes the narrative in your family and your community.

Final Word

Your culture shaped how you first viewed money. But your mindset will determine what you *do* with it. Don't let your past limit your future. Whether you come from privilege or pain, you have the right to financial literacy. You have the power to understand. And you have the responsibility to take control.

Because when you understand money, you don't just win on the field — you win in life.

Money = Options

Most people live paycheck to paycheck. Not because they're lazy or reckless—but because they never learned how to plan, save, and invest early. They get stuck working jobs they hate, signing bad contracts, or making decisions out of desperation instead of strategy.

When you save and invest now, you build a cushion—and that cushion gives you room to breathe. You won't have to take every deal just for the money. You can:

- Start your own business
- Go back to school
- Travel
- Help your family
- Support causes you care about
- Invest in real estate or other people's ideas

Saving money gives you time.

Investing money gives you leverage.

Together, they give you options.

Small Moves = Big Results

You don't need millions to start. You just need consistency.

Let's say you invest just $150/month starting at age 20. That's $1,800 a year—less than what many student-athletes make from a single NIL post. If you do that for 30 years and earn an average of 8% per year, you'll have around $220,000 by age 50.

If you increase that to $300/month? Now you're looking at over $440,000.

That's not even pro athlete money—it's future-proof money.

Your Future Self Will Thank You

When you're 20, the decisions you make might feel small. But they're not. You're laying the foundation. And just like training, reps now pay off later.

Imagine being 30 and having enough invested to take a year off to travel.

Imagine being 40 and owning two rental properties that generate passive income.

Imagine being 50 and choosing to work—or not—because you planned for it.

None of that happens by accident. It starts now, with the money you earn through NIL or summer jobs, and what you decide to do with it.

Final Word: The Sooner You Start, the More Choices You'll Have

Money isn't everything—but it makes everything easier when used wisely.

If you save and invest with discipline now, you'll have choices that most people only dream of.

Give your future self the gift of options.

Be the athlete today who builds the freedom to live life on your terms tomorrow.

Use NIL to Launch Your Next Career, Not Just a Lifestyle

Right now, you've got something rare: a platform, an audience, and income through NIL. You're building a brand, getting paid for your influence, and maybe even getting free gear, endorsements, and opportunities that most people your age never experience.

But here's the real question:

Are you using your NIL to build a lifestyle—or to launch a career?

Buying new clothes, traveling, upgrading your car—those things feel good in the moment. They give you that sense of success. But if the money stops tomorrow, does the progress stop too?

Lifestyle fades. Careers last.

NIL Isn't Just a Payday—It's a Platform

NIL deals aren't just checks—they're introductions. They're chances to connect with brands, CEOs, entrepreneurs, creators, alumni, and future business partners. If you're intentional, your NIL journey can double as a launchpad for whatever comes next.

Here's how:

- Turn partnerships into relationships

- Don't just take the check and disappear. Follow up. Thank the brand. Ask how else you can collaborate. Show you're about business, not just hype.
- Build a portfolio
- Every NIL campaign you do is a case study. Screenshot it. Save the stats. Create a digital résumé showing what you've done and the value you brought. That can lead to marketing jobs, consulting work, and future brand deals.
- Explore industries that interest you
- Like fitness? Partner with gyms and wellness companies.
- Into fashion? Work with apparel brands and learn the design or production side.
- Love content? Build your media brand and learn how editing, SEO, and monetization really work.

Use NIL to test-drive careers—not just to cash in.

Fund Your Future

Your NIL earnings can also help you:

- Start a business
- Pay for certifications or grad school
- Invest in real estate or a retirement account
- Hire a mentor or coach to level up your knowledge
- Take an unpaid internship you otherwise couldn't afford

Most people grind for years to save enough money to take these kinds of risks. You're in a position to do it now—if you're smart.

Your Career Starts Now

You don't have to wait until the game ends to figure out what's next. In fact, you shouldn't. The habits, relationships, and moves you make now will either open doors—or keep you scrambling when the lights go out.

You have a chance to walk out of college not just with a degree, but with a brand, a business, and a blueprint for what's next. That's what winning off the field really looks like.

Final Word: Cashing Out Is Cool—Cashing In on Your Future Is Smarter

You worked too hard to let NIL be just a moment.

Use it as a movement.

Build something that outlasts the trends.

Use NIL not just to live—use it to launch.

Conclusion: Winning Off the Field

You came into this book because you care about your future. You're not just here for the short-term wins—you're here to play the long game. And now, you've got the tools, the mindset, and the knowledge to do exactly that.

NIL has changed the landscape. It's opened doors that generations before you didn't have access to. You have opportunities to earn, to build, to brand, and to lead in ways most college students can only imagine. But with those opportunities come choices—and the way you handle those choices now will shape the rest of your life.

You've learned how to manage your money, track your income, avoid taxes hitting like a blindside blitz, and invest early so your future self has options. You've learned how to treat yourself like a business—not just an athlete—and how to build a support network, protect your brand, and plan for life after sports.

But more than that, you've learned that real success isn't about the moment—it's about what comes after it.

The wins that matter most won't be listed in box scores. They'll show up in the freedom you create for yourself.

- The freedom to walk away from bad deals
- The freedom to take a chance on your dream
- The freedom to support your family, your community, and yourself—without stress

That's what financial literacy is all about. It's not about being rich just to say you are.

It's about being in control—of your money, your time, your decisions, and your life.

Because when the last game ends, when the jersey comes off, when the followers slow down, and the cameras point elsewhere—you'll still be here. And how you prepared while the spotlight was on will determine what happens next.

You've already proven that you're dedicated. You've shown up to early morning lifts, pushed through tough practices, bounced back from setbacks, and stayed hungry when things got hard.

Now it's time to apply that same energy to your financial life.

To your business.

To your future.

Final Word: Your Legacy Is Bigger Than Your Stats

Your legacy won't just be what you did on the field. It'll be what you built after the game.

Will you be the athlete who blew the bag—or the one who flipped it into something that lasts?

Will you spend your NIL moment chasing clout—or building your career?

That choice is yours.

But remember this:

Winning off the field takes vision, discipline, and consistency—just like winning on it.

And if you're reading this, you already have what it takes.

So go be great.

Not just on game day—but every day.

This is your life. This is your brand. This is your legacy.

Now go win it. Off the field. For good.

Success Isn't a Highlight Reel—It's What Happens Off-Camera

We live in a world where it's easy to confuse success with attention.

You post a clip. It gets likes. You sign an NIL deal. You get followers. You score big in a game. You go viral. It *looks* like you're winning—and in many ways, you are.

But real success? The kind that lasts?

It happens off-camera.

It's what you do when no one's watching.

It's in the choices you make after the lights go out.

It's in the discipline of budgeting when the money hits your account.

It's in saying "no" to the shiny, short-term purchase so you can say "yes" to long-term freedom.

It's in the extra hour you spend learning how investing works, while others scroll past it.

Highlights are loud. They flash across screens and get reposted. But the real wins—the ones that build generational wealth, stability, peace of mind, and opportunity—those are quiet. Steady. Behind the scenes.

You're More Than the Clips

What the world sees:

- The brand deals
- The gear
- The followers
- The stats
- The smiles

What they don't see:

- You researching what a Roth IRA is
- You setting up a meeting with a financial advisor
- You saying no to that third trip this month because you're focused on saving
- You staying in to finish a pitch deck, write a business plan, or build your personal brand

That's the work that doesn't get likes—but it gets results.

Long-Term Success Is Built in the Shadows

Every legendary athlete has moments the fans never see. The late-night lifts. The rehab sessions. The quiet self-doubt. The film study after everyone else has gone home.

Your financial success is no different.

Every time you track your expenses, contribute to your investment account, or ask a mentor for guidance, you're stacking invisible wins. You're laying a foundation that doesn't show up on the timeline—but will show up when it matters most.

Final Thought: Chase Legacy, Not Just Hype

Don't get caught living for the highlight reel. Because once the game is over and the noise fades, what you're left with is what you built behind the scenes.

Money comes and goes. Trends fade. But discipline? Knowledge? Ownership?

Those things last.

So let others chase the flash.

You? Chase the foundation. The freedom. The future.

Because success isn't just the crowd cheering—it's the quiet moment when you look at your bank account, your business, your peace of mind, and you smile...

knowing you played the real game right.

Off-camera. Off the field.

And still winning.

Don't Take Advice from Just Anyone—Especially Not Your Uncle Who Teaches 7th Grade Math (No Offense)

Let's be real. Once you start making money, everyone suddenly becomes a financial expert.

Your teammate tells you to invest in crypto.

Your friend swears by some sketchy NFT.

Your uncle—who teaches 7th grade math and drives a 20-year-old minivan—starts talking to you about "flipping houses" and "how back in his day..."

Listen, no offense to your uncle. He's probably a great guy, a solid teacher, and someone who means well. But when it comes to managing NIL money, building wealth, or launching your business brand?

You need more than good intentions. You need expertise.

The Cost of Bad Advice

The wrong advice doesn't just waste your time—it can cost you thousands of dollars. It can delay your goals, ruin your credit, or leave you with a tax mess that takes years to fix.

Not everyone who cares about you knows what they're talking about when it comes to:

- Taxes and deductions
- Investment strategy
- LLC formation
- NIL contract terms
- Insurance coverage
- Budgeting for fluctuating income

Just because someone "heard it on YouTube" or "did it one time in the '90s" doesn't mean it applies to your situation in 2025.

Get Your Financial Advice from Real Professionals

You wouldn't let someone who's never played a down coach your team, right?

Then why take financial advice from someone who's never managed six-figure income, reviewed a contract, or filed a self-employment tax return?

When it comes to your money, your team matters.

Work with professionals who understand:

- NIL rules and regulations
- Student-athlete eligibility concerns

- Taxes for self-employed individuals
- How to help you plan for both now and the future

This includes:

- Certified Financial Planners (CFPs)
- CPAs with NIL or athlete experience
- NIL agents who've worked with other student-athletes
- Attorneys who specialize in contract and intellectual property law

You Can Still Love Your Uncle—Just Don't Bank on His Advice

Let the uncle teach math class. Let your teammate be hype on Instagram. Let your roommate invest in meme coins if they want.

But you? You're building something real.

Ask questions. Be curious. But always check the credentials.

Because when it comes to money, legacy, and long-term wealth, guessing isn't good enough.

Final Word: Respect Everyone. Listen to a Few. Choose the Right Ones.

Take advice from people who are where you want to be—not just people who talk loud.

This is your money, your brand, your future.

Get your game plan from pros, not just your people.

Surround Yourself with Professionals Who Know the Game

Every great athlete has a team behind the scenes: coaches, trainers, film guys, nutritionists, therapists, mentors—the people who don't make the highlight reel but make everything else possible.

Your financial life should be the same way.

You need a team.

Not just hype people, but professionals—advisors, accountants, attorneys, and mentors who understand your goals and know how to guide you through the game of money.

Because here's the truth:

Winning off the field takes a game plan—and the right people to help you execute it.

Not Everyone Knows the Athlete Life—But Some Do

You don't need a suit who's never touched a field telling you how to live.

You need someone who's been there. Someone who understands what it's like to juggle school, sports, pressure, and now, business.

Someone who's walked in your cleats—and still knows how to build wealth, structure deals, and protect your future.

That's where people like Pat Brown, MBA, come in.

Pat isn't just a money guy. He's a former Division I football player who knows what it's like to be in your shoes—and more importantly, what it takes to be successful once those shoes come off.

After competing at the highest levels and briefly playing professionally, Pat shifted his energy toward a different kind of game: helping student-athletes win with their money.

He's built multiple financial education platforms, speaks nationally to athletes, and is a trusted advocate for young people navigating the new NIL era. From budgeting and taxes to investing and entrepreneurship, Pat helps athletes like you move with strategy—not stress.

Who You Surround Yourself With = Who You Become

If you only take advice from people who are winging it, you'll end up winging it too.

But when you put smart, experienced people in your circle—people who understand NIL, contracts, money, and mindset—you position yourself to make moves, not mistakes.

The right people will help you:

- Avoid tax traps
- Invest wisely
- Protect your brand
- Start your business the right way
- Build wealth that lasts long after the cheers fade

This isn't about being flashy. It's about being future-ready.

Final Word: Find People Who Want You to Win Off the Field

Your success doesn't stop with the game—it starts when you build a life beyond it.

So surround yourself with pros who know the playbook. People who see you as more than a follower count or a stat sheet. Because champions aren't just made in the weight room.

They're built with wisdom, guidance, and the right team around them.

Keep Learning, Keep Growing, and Play to Win for Life

By now, you've realized something important: this game is bigger than sports.

Yes, you've trained your body, sharpened your skills, and competed at the highest levels. But the next stage of your journey? That's where your legacy is built.

Winning in life—*real life*—requires a new kind of playbook.

You've got to learn how money works.

You've got to protect what you're building.

You've got to prepare for the long game—not just the next paycheck, semester, or season.

But here's the best part: you already have everything inside you to do it.

You've shown up early. You've grinded. You've stayed disciplined when no one was watching. You've bounced back after losses. You've held yourself accountable.

Now, it's time to apply that same energy to your finances, your business moves, your relationships, and your mindset.

This Isn't a One-Time Play—It's a Lifelong Season

Financial literacy isn't something you learn once and forget.

It's something you practice. Just like your sport.

You're not going to master everything overnight. And that's okay. What matters is that you *keep learning*.

Keep asking questions.

Keep showing up.

Keep surrounding yourself with mentors, professionals, and people who want to see you win off the field.

No one is expecting you to be perfect. They're expecting you to be intentional.

Growth Is the Real Goal

Money will come and go. Followers rise and fall. Careers start and end.

But growth? That's forever.

The student-athlete who reads this book and takes action—starts saving, opens an investment account, asks for help, plans for life after the game—that person becomes the professional, the entrepreneur, the parent, the leader, the community builder.

That person becomes someone with options, ownership, and peace of mind.

That person becomes you.

Final Word: Play to Win for Life

You've learned what it takes to win on the field. You've pushed yourself. You've earned the right to be here.

Now it's time to take that same mindset and apply it to every area of your life.

NIL is just the beginning.

Money is just a tool.

Your sport is just one chapter.

But your life?

That's the big game.

So keep learning.

Keep growing.

Keep showing up.

And most of all—

Play to win. Not just today. Not just for likes.

Play to win for life.

You've got this. Let's go.

Chapter 14: Conversations With Your Parents About Money

"Talking about money doesn't divide us—it builds us."

As a student-athlete, you're in a unique position. You may be one of the first in your family to earn a real income while still in college. With NIL opportunities now on the table, you're managing things like branding, taxes, and bank accounts that most people don't deal with until much later in life—if at all.

But here's the thing: your success with money shouldn't be a solo mission. One of the most important moves you can make is to bring your parents or guardians into the conversation. Whether you were raised by a single mom who worked two jobs to keep the lights on or by two parents who modeled responsible financial behavior, having honest and healthy conversations about money can strengthen your path—and theirs.

Why These Conversations Matter

These talks aren't about asking for permission or proving you've got it all figured out. They're about connection, understanding, and creating a shared vision for the future.

- You're building financial habits that could shape your whole life.

- Your parents may be proud, concerned, or unsure how to help.
- You may be in a position to support your family—but you also need support yourself.
- Talking about money eliminates confusion and assumptions on both sides.

Let's Not Make Money Taboo

In many households, money is a sensitive topic. Maybe it was never talked about. Maybe it was a source of stress or tension. But silence doesn't help—it only creates shame or confusion.

Money is just a tool. Talking about it openly can bring clarity and opportunity for everyone involved.

Topics to Talk About With Your Parents

You don't have to cover all these at once. Start small, stay curious, and lead with respect. These conversations are a chance to grow as a family.

1. What Was Money Like Growing Up?

Ask:

- "What did you learn about money when you were younger?"
- "Was money talked about in your home?"
- "Were there things you had to figure out on your own?"

Understanding your parents' background with money can give you context for their values, fears, or habits.

2. What Are Our Family's Financial Goals?

Ask:

- "Are there goals we're working toward as a family?"
- "What would financial peace look like for us?"
- "How can my NIL opportunity support us—not just now, but long-term?"

This helps shift the conversation from short-term help to long-term planning.

3. How Can I Handle My NIL Income the Right Way?

Ask:

- "Can we build a budget together?"
- "Should I open my own bank account?"
- "Can we talk to someone together—like a financial coach or advisor?"

This approach invites your parents to grow with you and builds trust without giving up your independence.

4. What Monthly Bills or Financial Responsibilities Do We Have?

Ask:

- "Can you show me what our expenses look like each month?"
- "How do you manage bills and due dates?"
- "Is there anything I should start taking care of myself?"

When you understand what goes into running a household, you become more financially grounded and prepared.

5. What Should I Know About Credit?

Ask:

- "How did you first learn about credit?"
- "Have you ever had debt you had to overcome?"
- "What should I avoid as I start building my credit score?"

This conversation can prevent future mistakes and build healthy habits early on.

6. Do We Save or Invest? Should I Start?

Ask:

- "What's our approach to saving?"
- "Do we have anything set aside for emergencies?"
- "Would it make sense for me to start saving now or investing for the future?"

Even if your family hasn't saved much, starting this conversation can lead to powerful new habits—for everyone.

7. What Do You Wish You'd Known About Money?

Ask:

- "If you could go back and give your younger self financial advice, what would it be?"
- "What do you wish someone had taught you?"
- "What do you hope I don't have to learn the hard way?"

This question can create the deepest connection—because it's about wisdom, not just numbers.

If You Were Raised by a Single Parent

Let them know you see them.

Say things like:

- "I know you've done so much on your own. I want to be smart with my money to help, not add stress."
- "I'm learning about finances, and I'd love to include you in this process."

This isn't about replacing them—it's about growing together and honoring their sacrifices.

If Both Parents Are Involved and Financially Literate

Use their knowledge. They're one of your greatest assets.

Say things like:

- "You both know a lot about money. Can I show you what I'm learning?"
- "I want to make sure I'm not missing anything in my NIL planning."

You don't have to navigate NIL alone when your support system wants you to win.

Final Word: Talk With Love, Not Ego

This is not about impressing your family or defending your choices—it's about building something better, together.

Your NIL income is a starting point. Your relationship with your family is a foundation.

When you connect the two, you create not just wealth—but legacy.

Let the conversation begin.

Chapter 15: The Power of No – Protecting Your Peace and Your Pockets

Introduction: When the Checks Start Coming In, So Do the Requests

When the NIL money starts flowing, it's exciting. You're signing endorsement deals, making money through content, merchandise, appearances, and sponsorships. But just as real as the income is the pressure. The calls and texts start coming in. Family members you love ask for "just a little help." Friends expect you to cover dinner, buy gear, or invest in their "big idea." Old contacts come out of nowhere with financial needs or business pitches.

Saying "no" in these moments isn't being cold—it's being smart. It's not just about protecting money, it's about protecting your future, your mental health, and your peace of mind. This chapter will help you learn how to say no clearly, kindly, and confidently—without guilt.

Why It's Hard to Say "No"

Let's start with the truth: for many student-athletes, especially first-generation wealth earners, success isn't seen as just personal—it's a win for the entire family. It can feel like everyone is depending on you. Maybe you:

- Feel like the "chosen one" expected to lift everyone up
- Want to give back out of gratitude
- Feel guilty for having something others don't
- Think people won't understand if you say no

These emotions are valid. But always saying yes—especially when you can't afford to—doesn't help anyone in the long run. You didn't work hard just to become someone else's safety net. You worked hard to build a life of freedom and opportunity. Protect that.

The Real Cost of Always Saying Yes

Handing out money feels good in the short term. You feel generous. You feel needed. You feel like you're doing right by people who matter to you. But here's what often happens over time:

- Your finances start slipping—savings disappear, bills pile up, and you fall behind on your own goals.
- People get used to the handouts. What felt like help becomes an expectation.
- You find it hard to say no later. And when you finally do, people react negatively.
- Resentment grows. You feel used, and they feel entitled.

Always saying yes creates a pattern. You stop investing in yourself. You become the plan for everyone else. But who is helping you?

What to Say Instead of "No"

Saying "no" doesn't have to be rude or aggressive. You can communicate boundaries with kindness, clarity, and firmness. Here are some ways to say no—without feeling like a bad person:

- "I've already committed my money to a financial plan. Everything's accounted for."
- "I'm trying to build something that lasts. I can't give out money right now."
- "I've talked with my advisor, and right now I'm not in a position to help."
- "I love you, but I'm not loaning or gifting money to anyone right now."
- "I can't give you money, but I'm happy to support you in other ways."

Here's a tip: blame the plan, not the person. Instead of making it about their request being unreasonable, make it about your plan being the priority. You aren't rejecting them—you're sticking to your structure.

Enabling vs. Empowering

Let's say you help someone out. Maybe you pay a car note or cover rent one month. It feels good. But what happens next month? And the month after that?

If you give money without teaching financial skills, you're not helping—you're enabling. That means you're creating a dependency. Now, instead of solving a problem, you've just delayed it and trained someone to come to you again.

Empowering someone is different. It looks like:

- Helping them get a job or build a budget
- Encouraging them to learn about money
- Offering guidance instead of a handout
- Supporting their growth, not just their survival

Handouts end. Education multiplies.

You Are Not Their Financial Plan

If someone's entire financial recovery depends on *you*, that's a problem. You are not their emergency fund, retirement plan, or financial institution.

Here are some boundaries that protect you:

- No loans, no exceptions
- No gifts unless it's budgeted and doesn't hurt you
- No investing in someone else's business without full due diligence
- No cosigning or opening credit in your name for anyone

If you decide to help, do it intentionally and once—not habitually and out of guilt.

Legacy Over Likes

A lot of athletes fall into the trap of being liked. They want to be seen as generous, successful, and loyal. But being liked by everyone can leave you broke. What matters more than likes is legacy.

Legacy is what you leave behind—wealth, wisdom, and example. Protecting your money now means being able to:

- Buy your first home
- Invest in a business of your own
- Support your future kids
- Take care of your parents in retirement
- Give back to your community in bigger ways later

Saying no today might hurt someone's feelings. But saying yes and ending up broke helps no one.

When You're the First to Make It

Being the first in your family or community to have money is a beautiful but heavy role. You feel the pressure to give back. You feel the eyes on you. You feel like if you don't help, no one will.

But remember:

- You help people best when you're stable yourself.
- You can't give from an empty account.
- Just because you're first doesn't mean you're responsible for everyone else's success.

You can inspire others by showing what responsible money looks like. That example is worth more than any handout.

Boundaries Are Not Betrayal

Let's get something straight: saying no is not betrayal. It's self-respect. Setting boundaries doesn't make you cold, distant, or selfish. It means you know where your limits are.

Saying no now may mean fewer calls, fewer messages, or some awkward silence. That's okay. People who love you will understand. And if they don't, that tells you something too.

Boundaries protect your ability to keep showing up—for yourself, and one day, for others who *truly* need it.

Create a Script

Don't wait until you're put on the spot. Have a go-to response ready for when people ask for money.

Here's a script:

"I've created a financial plan for my income, and I'm not giving out any money right now. I hope you understand. I'm focused on building something long-term."

Or:

"I've made the decision not to lend or give money to friends or family. It's a personal boundary I'm holding to make sure I stay on track."

You can adjust the tone based on who you're talking to—but keep the boundary firm.

Help Without Giving Money

Sometimes you want to help—but not with cash. That's a great instinct. Here's how you can still be supportive:

- Recommend a job lead or resource
- Help someone budget or apply for assistance
- Introduce them to a mentor or advisor
- Give them books or podcasts on financial literacy
- Offer your time or emotional support instead

Money isn't the only way to care.

If You Do Say Yes, Do It Right

If you decide to help someone financially, set clear terms:

- Be specific about the amount
- Make it a one-time gift, not a recurring expectation
- If it's a loan, write it down and agree on a repayment timeline
- Say, "This is a one-time thing," and stick to it

Helping someone once doesn't mean you're now responsible for them. Be generous on your terms—not theirs.

Know the Red Flags

Some people won't take no for an answer. Watch for:

- Guilt-tripping: "But you owe me after everything I did for you."
- Pressure: "You have the money, why not help?"
- Repeated asks: "Just this one more time..."
- Manipulation: "If you really loved me, you'd do this."

These are signs someone may be more interested in your money than your well-being. Don't fall for it.

What Happens If You Don't Learn to Say No

Many athletes give and give—until there's nothing left.

They sign great deals, but they never build anything for themselves.

They support everyone except the one person who earned it: themselves.

Then the deals dry up. The attention fades. And the money's gone.

And suddenly, all the people who were always around... disappear.

Learn to say no now, so that when the spotlight dims, you're still standing on something solid.

Closing Thoughts: Say No Now, So You Can Say Yes Later

Saying no today protects your ability to say yes tomorrow.

Yes to a house.

Yes to investing.

Yes to giving generously—when you're in a place to do it.

Yes to building real wealth.

Yes to your own dreams.

Don't let short-term pressure ruin your long-term vision. You are not just someone's ATM. You are a brand, a business, and a future success story in the making.

Protect your peace. Guard your generosity. Lead with wisdom. And always remember: *"No" is a complete sentence.*

Chapter 16: The Eighth Wonder of the World – Understanding Compound Interest

Introduction: Why Time Is the Most Powerful Asset You Have

When it comes to building wealth, most people think it takes a lot of money. But the truth is, it takes **time and consistency** more than anything else. One of the most powerful forces in all of finance is **compound interest**—and the earlier you start using it, the more it works in your favor.

Albert Einstein allegedly called compound interest the "eighth wonder of the world." He supposedly said:

> *"He who understands it, earns it. He who doesn't, pays it."*

Whether or not Einstein actually said it doesn't matter—because the principle is *absolutely* true. Compound interest can make your NIL money grow exponentially over time, or it can work against you if you're borrowing and building debt.

In this chapter, you'll learn what compound interest is, how it works, how to make it your financial superpower, and how to avoid being crushed by it through credit cards, loans, or missed opportunities.

What Is Compound Interest?

Compound interest is interest that earns interest. You make money not just on your original investment (called the "principal"), but also on the interest that investment earns over time.

Unlike simple interest, which only pays on the principal, compound interest grows faster and faster over time because every year, you're earning interest on a bigger number.

It's like a snowball rolling downhill—slow at first, but eventually unstoppable.

Example:

If you invest $1,000 at 10% annual interest:

- **Year 1**: You earn $100. Now you have $1,100.
- **Year 2**: You earn $110 (10% of $1,100). Now you have $1,210.
- **Year 3**: You earn $121. Now you have $1,331.

Over time, the gains get bigger—not because you added more money, but because the growth builds on itself.

Why Compound Interest Matters for You (Especially Now)

You have something most people don't: **youth**. And when it comes to compound interest, the earlier you start, the more powerful it becomes.

Even small amounts can turn into huge sums if you give them time.

Let's compare two athletes:

- **Athlete A** starts investing $200/month at age 18 and stops at age 28. She invests for just 10 years—$24,000 total.
- **Athlete B** waits until age 28 to start and invests $200/month until age 65. He invests for 37 years—$88,800 total.

Assuming an 8% return, who ends up with more money at 65?

Answer: Athlete A, who started earlier, ends up with more money—*even though she invested for fewer years and less money*—because her money had more time to grow.

Time Is More Valuable Than Timing

A lot of people try to "time the market." They wait for the right moment to invest. But when it comes to compound interest, time **in** the market matters far more than trying to time the market.

The best time to start was yesterday. The second-best time is today.

The longer your money stays invested, the more compound interest can do its magic.

Rule of 72 – The Shortcut to Doubling Your Money

Want to know how long it takes to double your money with compound interest? Use the **Rule of 72**.

Just divide 72 by your expected annual return.

For example:

- 72 ÷ 6% = 12 years to double
- 72 ÷ 9% = 8 years to double
- 72 ÷ 12% = 6 years to double

So if you earn 9% annually, your money will double about every 8 years. That means $10,000 becomes $20,000 in 8 years… $40,000 in 16 years… and $80,000 in 24 years. Without you adding a single extra dollar.

The Compounding Timeline – Why Waiting Hurts

Here's the key: **every year you wait makes it harder to catch up.** Let's look at three athletes who all invest $100/month at 8% return.

- **Start at age 18**: $100/month = ~$351,428 by age 65
- **Start at age 28**: ~$164,870 by age 65
- **Start at age 38**: ~$74,336 by age 65

Waiting just 10 years can cost you hundreds of thousands of dollars. That's the power of compound interest. It rewards early starters and punishes procrastinators.

Where Can You Use Compound Interest?

You don't need to be a Wall Street trader to benefit from compounding. Here are common accounts that allow compound interest to work for you:

- **Roth IRA** – Tax-free growth and withdrawals in retirement
- **Traditional IRA or 401(k)** – Tax-deferred growth
- **High-yield savings accounts** – Low growth, but still compound
- **Investment accounts (brokerage accounts)** – Stocks, ETFs, mutual funds
- **HSA (Health Savings Account)** – Triple tax benefit if used properly

Start small. Stay consistent. Let time do the heavy lifting.

Compound Interest Can Hurt You Too

So far we've talked about compound interest working *for* you. But it can also work *against* you—especially when you're dealing with **debt**.

Credit cards, payday loans, and high-interest loans compound your **debt**, not your wealth.

Let's say you owe $5,000 on a credit card at 22% interest. If you don't pay it off quickly, that balance can balloon. You end up paying thousands more than you borrowed.

The same snowball effect that makes investments grow can turn debt into a financial disaster.

Protect Yourself: Avoid the Trap of Reverse Compounding

To make compound interest work for you, not against you:

- **Pay off credit cards** in full each month
- **Avoid payday loans** or high-interest borrowing
- **Don't finance things you don't need**
- **Invest early and regularly**—even small amounts matter
- **Automate savings and investment** to stay consistent

The goal is to **earn** compound interest, not **owe** it.

The Mindset Shift: Think Like an Investor, Not a Spender

Here's the bottom line: when you get NIL money, you'll be tempted to **spend it**. That's natural. But every dollar you spend today is a dollar that won't grow tomorrow.

Think like an investor. Ask:

- Will this help me grow long-term?
- Am I giving this dollar a job, or am I letting it disappear?
- Can I invest this now so I don't have to work as hard later?

Compound interest is like planting a tree. You won't get shade immediately—but in a few years, you'll be thankful you did.

How to Get Started – Action Steps

1. **Open a Roth IRA** – It's tax-free growth, and you can contribute up to $6,500/year (as of 2025) if you have earned income.
2. **Set up recurring contributions** – Automate $50, $100, or more monthly.
3. **Choose a low-cost index fund** – S&P 500 or Total Market index funds are great for starters.
4. **Leave it alone** – Resist the urge to withdraw. Let it compound.
5. **Check once a year** – Rebalance if needed, but don't obsess.
6. **Increase contributions as your income grows** – Pay yourself first.

Final Thoughts: Make Compound Interest Your Teammate

As a student-athlete, you understand what it means to play the long game. You show up, you train, and the results come later. Compound interest works the same way.

It rewards patience, discipline, and consistency.

The money you invest now has the power to buy your freedom later—freedom to choose your job, support your family, travel, give back, and retire early.

So don't just hustle for NIL money today. **Put some of it to work for the future you.**

Compound interest doesn't need you to be rich to start.

It just needs you to start.

Chapter 17: What's a Portfolio? Build Your Game Plan, Diversify Your Lineup

Every Athlete Needs a Game Plan

Think of your financial future like a championship season. You wouldn't hit the court or field without a playbook, right? You need strategy. You need roles. You need a team that can win in different situations.

That's exactly what a **portfolio** is. It's your financial lineup. It's a mix of different players—investments—each with their own strengths, risks, and jobs to do. When you build a smart portfolio, you're giving yourself the best shot at long-term success.

So, What's in a Portfolio?

A portfolio is your mix of money moves. It includes things like:

- Stocks (your offensive players – high-scoring, high-risk)
- Bonds (your defense – stable, dependable, protects the lead)
- Cash (your bench – ready when you need quick subs or timeouts)
- Real estate, ETFs, mutual funds (your utility players – all-around options)

Just like you wouldn't play a whole basketball game with only point guards, you don't want your financial team made up of one type of investment.

You need balance. You need different players. That's where **diversification** comes in.

Why Diversification Is Like Having a Strong Team

If you put your entire financial future into one stock or one type of investment, it's like betting the whole season on one player. What if they get injured? What if they have a bad game? You're cooked.

Diversification is spreading out your risk. It's like building a full roster—scorers, defenders, role players—so if one guy has a bad night, others can step up.

When the market gets rough (and it will), your diversified portfolio helps you stay in the game.

Different Portfolio "Teams" – Conservative, Moderate, Aggressive

Depending on your goals, age, and mindset, you're going to want a different type of portfolio "team." Let's break it down.

Conservative Portfolio – Play Defense First

This is the type of lineup you build when protecting the lead matters more than running up the score.

You're stacking your team with safe, slow-moving players: mostly bonds, with a few stocks sprinkled in.

It's like playing zone defense, controlling the tempo, limiting fast breaks. You're not trying to blow anyone out—you're just trying not to lose.

Who's it for?

- Athletes close to retirement

- People who need their money soon
- Anyone with a low risk tolerance

Pros:

- Less volatile
- Easier to sleep at night
- Steady, predictable returns

Cons:

- Less upside
- May not beat inflation
- Not ideal for young players building wealth

Moderate Portfolio – Balanced Offense and Defense

This is your two-way team. A good mix of offense (stocks) and defense (bonds).

You've got players who can score, but you're not ignoring protection. It's like a team that can grind out close games and still run when they need to.

Who's it for?

- Athletes with 5–10 year goals
- Those who want growth but hate chaos
- Anyone building wealth and playing it smart

Pros:

- Balanced risk and return
- Can handle market swings better
- Suitable for most people in the middle of their career

Cons:

- Can feel slow when the market's hot
- Still risky in downturns
- Requires patience

Aggressive Portfolio – Go For the Win

This is your fast-paced, high-scoring team. Mostly made up of stocks, it's built to run the floor, attack constantly, and take big swings.

It's not for the faint of heart—but over time, this strategy usually puts the most points on the board.

Who's it for?

- Young athletes
- People who won't need their money for 10+ years
- Risk-takers who understand the long game

Pros:

- Huge upside potential
- Great for early wealth building
- Takes full advantage of compounding over time

Cons:

- Big mood swings (a.k.a. market drops)
- Emotionally tough to stick with
- Not for short-term goals

How to Choose Your Strategy – When to Attack, When to Hold Back

Just like in sports, you change your game plan depending on the situation. You don't full-court press up 30 points in the fourth quarter. You don't play conservative if you're down 10 with two minutes left.

Same with investing.

Be more aggressive when:

- You're in your 20s and 30s
- You don't need the money for at least 10 years
- You're focused on building, not protecting
- You can handle the emotional swings of the market

Be more conservative when:

- You're close to needing the money (within 5 years)
- You're about to retire
- You're risk-averse and losing money keeps you up at night
- You've already won financially and just want to protect your lead

Your Portfolio Changes With Your Season

Your investing strategy should evolve just like your athletic career.

Early in your career? You're trying to grow, build, and take some smart risks. That's your aggressive portfolio phase.

Mid-career? You're balancing growth with protection. That's your moderate stage.

Later in life? You've built your lead—now it's about not blowing it. That's when you go conservative.

The key is to know where you are in the game and adjust your lineup accordingly.

Final Thoughts – Build a Dynasty, Not a One-Season Wonder

A good coach knows it's not just about winning one game—it's about building a program that lasts. Your portfolio is your program.

Don't get distracted by hype plays. Don't panic during a losing streak. Don't chase risky trades just because someone else hit big.

Stick to the fundamentals:

- Diversify your roster
- Match your strategy to your season
- Adjust over time
- Play the long game

Because when you look back after 10, 20, 30 years... you'll be glad you didn't go for just highlight reels. You built something solid.

You didn't just play the game.

You *owned* the league.

Chapter 18: Wrong Examples

here are several **real-world examples of athletes who made millions and then lost it all (or most of it)** due to poor financial decisions, lack of guidance, or unsustainable lifestyles. These stories can serve as powerful teaching tools in your book or workshops to show the importance of planning, saying "no," and building wealth the right way.

1. Allen Iverson – NBA

Estimated career earnings: Over $200 million

What happened: Lavish spending, generosity to friends and family, and a divorce drained his bank account. He was known for flying his crew on private jets, buying dozens of cars, and spending tens of thousands at a time in malls. He once reportedly refused to fly commercial—even for one night.

How he bounced back: Fortunately, Reebok had a **$32 million trust** set aside for him that he can access at age 55. That move likely saved his financial future.

2. Antoine Walker – NBA

Estimated career earnings: $108 million

What happened: Walker invested in failed real estate deals, supported over 70 friends and family members, and lived a high-spending lifestyle with luxury cars, jewelry, and gambling. He filed for bankruptcy just two years after retiring.

Lesson: Even $100 million isn't enough if you don't set boundaries and manage wisely.

3. Vince Young – NFL

Estimated career earnings: Around $35 million

What happened: Young famously spent $5,000 a week at The Cheesecake Factory and once bought every seat on a Southwest Airlines flight—just so he could fly alone. He trusted the wrong people, didn't track spending, and filed for bankruptcy in 2014.

4. Delonte West – NBA

Estimated career earnings: $16 million

What happened: After a solid NBA career, West faced mental health struggles and poor financial decisions. At one point, he was seen homeless and panhandling. His story is heartbreaking and reminds us that financial literacy and mental health go hand in hand.

Current status: With support from former teammate Mark Cuban, West entered rehab and has been working to rebuild his life.

5. Bernie Kosar – NFL

Estimated career earnings: Over $20 million

What happened: Kosar tried to help too many people. He once said he had **60 checking accounts** and over **50 real estate partnerships**, most of which failed. He gave away money without structure and later filed for bankruptcy.

Lesson: You can't save everyone. If you're everyone's emergency fund, you'll go broke trying to play hero.

6. Lenny Dykstra – MLB

Estimated career earnings: $36 million

What happened: After retirement, Dykstra lived lavishly and pursued risky business ventures with borrowed money. He declared bankruptcy in 2009 and was later sentenced to prison for bankruptcy fraud and money laundering.

Lesson: Taking financial risks without a plan can cost you more than just money—it can take your freedom.

7. Mike Tyson – Boxing

Estimated career earnings: $400+ million

What happened: Lavish spending on mansions, exotic animals (he once owned three Bengal tigers), luxury cars, and a massive entourage led Tyson to bankruptcy in 2003. He admitted to spending **$1 million per month at one point**.

Current status: Tyson has made a successful comeback through podcasting, entertainment, and cannabis ventures.

Lesson: It's not about how much you make—it's how much you keep.

8. JaMarcus Russell – NFL

Estimated career earnings: $40 million

What happened: Russell signed one of the biggest rookie contracts in NFL history but had little structure or financial discipline. He reportedly spent heavily on jewelry, cars, and poor investments. He never became a consistent starter, and his money didn't last.

Lesson: Earning potential doesn't matter if you don't have a financial game plan.

9. Sheryl Swoopes – WNBA

Estimated career earnings: Millions through salary and endorsements

What happened: Despite being a pioneer in women's basketball, Swoopes filed for bankruptcy in 2004. She made poor investment decisions, including trusting the wrong advisors and business ventures that failed.

Lesson: Even trailblazers need financial education and trusted guidance.

10. Evander Holyfield – Boxing

Estimated career earnings: Over $200 million

What happened: Holyfield bought a 109-room mansion, fathered 11 children with multiple women (with huge child support obligations), and had extravagant spending habits. He lost his home to foreclosure and faced serious financial setbacks.

Lesson: Lifestyle inflation and unchecked generosity can drain even the biggest bank accounts.

Final Thoughts

These examples aren't just cautionary tales—they're reminders of how fast money can disappear without a plan. Whether you're earning $10K or $10 million from NIL deals, you need:

- A budget
- A plan
- Financial boundaries
- Trusted advisors
- A long-term mindset

Learn from their mistakes—so your story can be one of legacy, not loss.

Chapter 19: How to Start Investing – Your NIL Playbook for Building Wealth

Introduction: Don't Just Get Paid. Build Something With It.

You just got that first big NIL check. Maybe it's $1,000, maybe it's $100,000. Either way, it's tempting to celebrate big—buy that new chain, take the trip, flex on the 'Gram. But real flex? Financial security. Long-term wealth. Getting your money to make more money.

That's what **investing** is all about. And the earlier you start, the stronger your financial game becomes. This chapter walks you through the play-by-play of how to start investing, how to choose the right kind of account, and how to make a smart plan for your NIL income—even if that first deal is massive.

Step 1: Understand What Investing Actually Is

Investing means putting your money to work so it can grow over time.

Instead of just sitting in a checking account (or getting spent on shoes and takeout), that money goes into stocks, bonds, ETFs, or mutual funds—assets that increase in value and pay you back in the future.

If you invest consistently, even small amounts can turn into big results over time. That's the power of compound interest (which we already talked about in another chapter).

Step 2: Know Your Goals and Time Frame

Before investing, ask yourself:

- When will I need this money?
- Am I okay if it goes up and down in the short term?
- Am I building wealth for the long game, or trying to flip it fast?

If you won't need the money for at least **5 years**, investing is usually a smart move. If you'll need it sooner (like for tuition, rent, or a car), keep that portion in cash.

Step 3: Choose Your Investment Account

Not all accounts are the same. The account **type** determines how your money is taxed and what rules apply. Here's the breakdown:

Roth IRA

- Funded with **after-tax** money
- Grows **tax-free**
- Withdrawals in retirement are **100% tax-free**
- Annual contribution limit: $6,500 (as of 2025)
- Must have **earned income** to contribute
- Great for student-athletes with NIL income who qualify based on income

Why it's great: Perfect for young people. You're in a low tax bracket now, so paying taxes up front means you never have to pay taxes on that money again—**ever.**

Traditional IRA

- Contributions may be **tax-deductible**
- Money grows tax-deferred
- You pay taxes when you withdraw later
- Same contribution limit: $6,500
- Income limits apply for deductions

Best for: Athletes who want a tax break now and expect to be in a lower tax bracket in retirement.

Taxable Brokerage Account

- No contribution limits
- No income restrictions
- Pay taxes on dividends, interest, and gains
- Full flexibility—you can pull money out whenever

Best for: Building wealth beyond the IRA cap. Also good for shorter-term investments you might use before retirement.

SEP IRA (Simplified Employee Pension IRA)

- For **self-employed** people or entrepreneurs (yes, that includes YOU if you run your NIL brand like a business)
- Contribute up to **25% of your net earnings**, up to $66,000 (as of 2025)
- Contributions are tax-deductible
- Grows tax-deferred

Best for: Student-athletes earning six figures from NIL, running their brand through an LLC, and wanting to stash away large amounts.

SIMPLE IRA (Savings Incentive Match Plan for Employees)

- Mostly for small businesses with employees
- Student-athletes might use this if they've launched a company or agency and hire others
- Contribution limit: $16,000 plus employer match
- Also grows tax-deferred

Best for: High-earning NIL athletes running a business with a few teammates or staffers

Step 4: The $100,000 NIL Check — Sample Breakdown

Let's say you just got **a $100,000 NIL check**. That's major. But here's how you turn that income into a launchpad—not a liability.

Step 1: Set aside taxes

If you're not having taxes withheld, assume **30%** for federal, state, and self-employment taxes.

$100,000 × 30% = $30,000 set aside for taxes

Put this in a separate account and don't touch it.

Step 2: Fund a Roth IRA

You qualify (assuming you're under the income limit), so take full advantage.

Max Roth IRA = $6,500

Invest it in a diversified stock index fund like the S&P 500. That money will grow tax-free for decades.

Step 3: Invest in a taxable brokerage account

You've still got plenty of money left. Let's invest more for the long haul.

Put $30,000–$40,000 into a brokerage account

Pick diversified ETFs or index funds. This money is flexible—you can tap it before retirement, but it'll still grow.

Step 4: Keep some cash on hand

Life happens. You need a cushion.

Set aside $10,000–$15,000 in a high-yield savings account

This is your emergency fund. If something breaks, you get hurt, or NIL slows down, you have backup.

Step 5: Give yourself a little room to enjoy

You're young. You earned it. Don't go crazy, but it's okay to enjoy a piece of it.

Spend $5,000–$10,000 guilt-free

Just know that fun money is capped. A budgeted reward is still responsible.

Recap of that $100K Game Plan:

- $30,000 for taxes
- $6,500 into a Roth IRA
- $35,000 into a brokerage account
- $15,000 in cash savings
- $8,500 to spend and celebrate

Now you've celebrated **and** set yourself up for long-term success. That's how a pro handles NIL money.

Step 5: Set It and Stay Consistent

Even if you don't have $100,000, the process is the same:

- Save for taxes
- Invest what you can
- Build a cash cushion
- Budget for spending
- Do it consistently

Use auto-transfers. Pick simple, low-cost investments like ETFs. Reinvest your dividends. Stick to your plan.

Final Thoughts: Don't Let a One-Time Check Be Your Only Win

NIL money can change your life—but only if you treat it like the start of something bigger.

Start investing now, even if it's just $100 a month. The earlier you start, the less you'll have to work later. Don't wait until you're "rich." Wealth isn't about what you make. It's about what you **keep** and what you **grow**.

Let your money run plays for you while you're grinding on and off the field.

Because true success?

It's not just winning today.

It's building a future you can live off forever.

Chapter 20: Helping Without Hurting – How to Support Loved Ones Without Going Broke

You Love Them. But You Can't Save Them All.

Let's talk about one of the hardest parts of coming into money—especially NIL money when you're young and the first in your family to earn like this.

Helping a single mom who's always held it down? You want to.

Helping your dad who's always struggled but showed up for your games? Feels like the least you can do.

Supporting a friend who's stuck or down bad? They were with you before the spotlight.

You want to be loyal. You want to be generous. You don't want to seem selfish.

But if you're not careful, you'll **drown while trying to save everyone else**.

This chapter is about doing it differently. About **helping without hurting**. About giving with **boundaries**, not guilt. About building a future where you don't have to say, "I used to have money..."

Start With This Truth: You're Not Their Retirement Plan

If you're earning NIL money and you're the first in the family to "make it," people will look to you for support. Sometimes it's asked for. Sometimes it's expected silently. Either way, you need a plan before you get pulled into financial chaos.

You are not your family's emergency fund.

You are not the government.

You are not a bottomless pit of money.

Even if you choose to help—**it has to be structured**.

Option 1: The Monthly Budget Strategy

Let's say you want to help Mom with groceries, bills, or rent. Instead of saying "yes" every time she calls, you set a **monthly family support budget.**

Example:

You decide $500 a month is what you can afford to help with **consistently** without sacrificing your own savings, investments, or goals.

Here's how that looks:

- $200 goes toward groceries or utilities
- $200 is paid directly to her landlord or mortgage company
- $100 goes on a pre-loaded debit card for other needs

Once you hit that $500 for the month, **you're done.**

If someone asks for more?

You say:

> *"I already hit my family support budget for the month. We can revisit it next month, but I can't go over that."*

You're not being cold—you're sticking to your boundaries.

Option 2: The Lump Sum Strategy

Maybe you don't want to deal with monthly requests. Maybe you want to give a little breathing room up front.

That's when you decide to **give a one-time gift**, and that's it.

Example:

You get a $20,000 NIL deal. You decide you can spare $2,000 to help Mom with overdue bills or car repairs.

You say:

> *"This is a one-time gift. I love you and wanted to do something meaningful. But after this, I won't be able to give more right now."*

Then you send it. You don't revisit. You don't fall into guilt. You protect your plan.

And here's the most important part: **you don't keep reloading the gift.**

This isn't a subscription service. It's one-time support—done with love and limits.

If It's More Than One Person…

What if you're trying to help your mom *and* your dad *and* your siblings *and* your childhood best friend who's "just tryna get back on their feet"?

Same rules. Set a **total monthly or annual support budget**, and divide it—if you want.

Example: You decide to budget $6,000 for family/friend support per year. That's $500/month total.

- Mom gets $300
- Dad gets $100
- Your best friend gets $100

That's it.

You don't add more. You don't loan more. You don't get drawn into guilt.

If one person's situation changes, it doesn't automatically mean your budget does.

Your **financial plan comes first**. Everyone else fits within that plan—or not at all.

Say It Early, Say It Often

If you don't say **how** and **how much** you're willing to help, people will assume it's unlimited. And assumptions are where resentment and entitlement grow.

Have the conversation. It might be awkward, but it's worth it.

You say:

> *"I love you, and I'm proud to be in a place to help. But I'm setting a boundary. I've got a budget for support, and once I hit that number, I can't go past it. It's not personal—it's me protecting my future."*

And when they say "but just this one time..."

You hold the line.

How to Avoid Enabling

Helping becomes **enabling** when:

- They stop trying to help themselves
- They start expecting it
- They guilt you when you say no
- You give money that solves the same problem over and over again
- You feel resentment instead of peace

To avoid enabling, try this:

- Pay the bill directly, don't give cash
- Offer help with job searching, not just money
- Suggest financial literacy resources
- Make the help temporary, not open-ended

If they need $200 for rent every month, what they really need is a plan, not a handout. You can love someone without being their financial crutch.

If They Get Mad, That's Okay

Boundaries make people uncomfortable—especially if they're used to you saying "yes."

They may accuse you of changing.

They may say, "You forgot where you came from."

They may try guilt or shame.

Let them.

Because the goal isn't to win everyone's approval.

The goal is to build something that lasts—for you and for the people you'll be able to help down the line **the right way**.

You can't pour into others if your own cup is empty.

Final Thoughts: Help With Strategy, Not Emotion

You're not heartless for saying no.

You're not selfish for setting limits.

You're not wrong for wanting to keep what you earned.

If you *choose* to help family or friends, do it:

- With intention
- With a clear budget
- With hard boundaries
- Without shame

Because the best gift you can give isn't a check.

It's the example of financial strength, discipline, and long-term thinking.

If they love you, they'll understand.

And if they don't now... they will when you're still standing strong ten years from now while others are broke and bitter.

That's real love. That's real leadership. That's legacy.

Chapter 21: What Is the Market, the Economy, and Everything Else You See on TV? (Explained with Sports Analogies)

You've probably heard things like:

"The market is crashing!"
"The S&P 500 is on a hot streak!"
"The Fed raised interest rates again!"
"Inflation is out of control!"

It's enough to make you want to change the channel.

But guess what? Once you understand what all this means, you'll see it's **just like a game**. The financial world has teams, scores, momentum, injuries, coaches, rules, and streaks — just like sports.

Let's break it all down so you can start playing to win.

What Exactly Is the Stock Market?

The **stock market** is where people **buy and sell shares of companies**. Buying a share means you own a small piece of a business like Nike, Apple, or Amazon.

Sports analogy: It's like being part of a franchise. You're not just a fan — you're a partial owner of the team. When the team wins and grows in value, so does your share.

What Causes the Market to Go Up or Down?

The stock market moves based on **supply and demand**.

If more people want to **buy**, prices go up.

If more people want to **sell**, prices go down.

What changes that supply and demand? News, earnings reports, interest rates, political events, and even tweets.

Sports analogy: Think of it like player hype. A good performance (great earnings) drives up value. A scandal or slump? The price drops fast.

What's the Difference Between the Stock Market and the Economy?

- The **market** is the scoreboard — investors' expectations about the future.
- The **economy** is the actual game — jobs, production, consumer spending, etc.

They're connected, but not the same.

Sports analogy: The market is fantasy football. The economy is the actual football game. Sometimes the fantasy points and the real game align — and sometimes they don't.

Is the Market Risky? Can I Lose All My Money?

Yes, there's risk. If you invest in **one stock**, it could crash. But if you invest in **hundreds of companies** through an index fund or ETF, your risk drops big time.

Sports analogy: Betting on one player is risky. Building a whole roster gives you protection. If one player flops, your team can still win.

What's the Best Way to Invest?

For most people, the best play is:

- **Index funds or ETFs** (which include hundreds of companies)
- **Roth IRA or brokerage account**
- **Long-term mindset**
- **Stay consistent**

Sports analogy: It's like running the offense — simple, repeatable, and hard to stop. You don't need trick plays. Just execute the fundamentals.

When's the Best Time to Start?

Now. Always now.

The earlier you start, the more time your money has to grow.

Sports analogy: The best athletes don't wait until playoffs to train. They build in the offseason. The earlier you invest, the stronger your financial "season" will be.

What's the S&P 500?

It's a list of the **500 biggest U.S. companies**, and it's used as a scoreboard to measure how the market is doing.

Sports analogy: Think of it as the AP Top 25 of business. If most companies in the S&P 500 are "winning," the market is doing well.

What's a Bull Market vs. a Bear Market?

- **Bull Market** = Prices rising, people feeling confident
- **Bear Market** = Prices falling 20% or more, people panicking

Sports analogy: A bull market is a winning streak — everything's clicking.

A bear market is a slump — the team's struggling, fans are frustrated.

Should I Sell When the Market Drops?

No. Selling during a drop locks in your losses.

Sports analogy: You don't bench your franchise player after one bad quarter. You ride it out, adjust, and stay focused on the long game.

How Much Money Do I Need to Start?

You can start with **$50, $100 — whatever you've got.** Many platforms let you buy **fractional shares** of big stocks.

Sports analogy: You don't have to start as the star. You just need to get on the roster. Reps build results.

Can I Make Fast Money in the Market?

Sure — but it's gambling. Not investing.

Day trading = playing hero ball.

Investing = running the system.

Sports analogy: Anyone can hit a half-court shot once. But champions win with consistent layups, defense, and smart plays.

What's an ETF?

An **ETF (Exchange-Traded Fund)** is a bundle of investments (like stocks or bonds) that you can buy or sell like one single stock.

Sports analogy: It's like drafting an entire all-star team with one pick. You don't have to guess which player will shine — you get them all.

Is Investing Only for Rich People?

Absolutely not.

Investing is for anyone who wants to build wealth. You don't need to start big — you just need to start.

Sports analogy: Great careers begin in high school gyms, not in pro arenas. Start where you are.

What's the Difference Between a Stock and a Bond?

- **Stock = ownership in a company**
- **Bond = loan to a company or government**

Stocks can grow more but are riskier. Bonds are steadier but slower.

Sports analogy: Stocks are like shooting guards — high-scoring, high risk. Bonds are like veteran defenders — low flash, but reliable.

What's Diversification?

Diversification means spreading your money across **lots of different investments** — not putting all your eggs in one basket.

Sports analogy: You don't build a team with only point guards. You need size, speed, shooters, defense — balance is the key to winning.

Why Do People Say "Buy Low, Sell High"?

Because that's how you make money: buy when prices are low, sell when they're higher.

But most people do the opposite — they panic when prices drop and buy when hype is high.

Sports analogy: You don't trade away your superstar when they're cold — you trust they'll bounce back.

How Do I Know What to Invest In?

Start simple:

- Index funds like S&P 500
- Total Market ETFs
- Low fees
- Wide diversification
- Reinvest dividends
- Stay long term

Sports analogy: You don't have to shoot from half-court. Just run the offense, take high-percentage shots, and play disciplined ball.

What Happens in a Recession?

A **recession** is when the economy slows down for several months.

Jobs get cut. People spend less. Businesses tighten up.

The market might drop — but it's usually temporary.

Sports analogy: A recession is a rebuilding year. No playoffs this season, but you use it to regroup and reload for the next run.

Do I Need a Financial Advisor?

Not to start. You can use apps like:

- Fidelity
- Vanguard
- Schwab
- M1 Finance
- Public
- Betterment

But if your NIL money grows, or your situation gets complex, a good **financial advisor** can be your coach.

What's the #1 Rule of Investing?

Start early. Stay consistent. Don't panic.

Sports analogy: The best players aren't perfect — they're dependable. They show up to every practice, stick to the playbook, and never get rattled by one loss.

What's a Dividend?

A **dividend** is a cash payout some companies give to their shareholders — a bonus just for being on the team.

Sports analogy: It's like getting a check even when you're on the bench. You don't have to do anything extra — just hold the stock and let it pay you.

How Often Should I Check My Investments?

Once a month. Maybe once a quarter.

Sports analogy: Checking your account every hour is like staring at the scoreboard during warmups. Focus on playing the game — not watching every score change.

What's a Stock Split?

When a stock gets expensive, companies sometimes **split** the shares to make them more affordable.

If you owned 1 share at $100, now you might own 2 shares at $50.

Sports analogy: It's like switching jersey numbers — the look changes, but your role on the team stays the same.

What's a Market Correction?

When the market drops about **10% from a recent high**, that's a **correction**.

It's normal and healthy — just part of the game.

Sports analogy: A correction is like a team huddle at halftime after a rough second quarter. Not a meltdown. Just time to refocus.

Should I Invest if the Market Is Going Down?

Yes. That's often the **best time** to invest — everything's on sale.

Sports analogy: It's like getting your favorite sneakers at 30% off. Same product. Just a better deal.

Can I Lose All My Money in the Market?

If you put everything into one stock? Yes.

If you invest in diversified funds or ETFs? **Very unlikely**.

Even during crashes, the total market has always bounced back.

Sports analogy: One player can get injured. But a deep bench? That keeps you in the game.

What's a Mutual Fund vs. an ETF?

Both are baskets of stocks or bonds.

- **Mutual funds**: trade once per day, may have higher fees
- **ETFs**: trade like stocks all day, usually cheaper and more flexible

Most beginners stick with ETFs.

Sports analogy: Mutual funds are like old-school coaches — still useful, but a bit slower. ETFs are today's fast-paced game — lean, simple, efficient.

What Are Interest Rates and Why Do They Matter?

Interest rates are the cost of borrowing money.

When the **Fed raises rates**, loans (like car loans, mortgages, business loans) get more expensive. That slows spending — which can hurt company profits — and cause the market to drop.

Sports analogy: It's like your coach making you run extra sprints. The whole team slows down. But sometimes it's necessary to build long-term stamina.

What's Dollar-Cost Averaging?

It means you invest the same amount of money on a regular schedule — no matter what the market's doing.

For example: $200/month into your Roth IRA, every month.

This strategy helps you buy more shares when prices are low and fewer when prices are high — averaging it out over time.

Sports analogy: It's like showing up to lift every week — no matter how tired you feel or how good last week was. The consistency is what wins.

Final Thoughts: Learn the Game. Play it Smart. Build Your Legacy.

The market isn't magic. The economy isn't a mystery. It's just a different version of a game you already understand.

- Diversify your portfolio like you build a team.
- Invest consistently like you train in the offseason.
- Don't panic during slumps.
- Stay calm during hype.
- Play the long game.

Because money, like sports, rewards discipline, patience, and preparation.

So put in your reps. Stick to the game plan.
And build a financial legacy that outlasts the spotlight.

Chapter 22: In Closing: From NIL to Legacy – The Journey Is Just Beginning

1. You're Not Just Making Money. You're Making History.

When you signed your first NIL deal, something shifted — not just for you, but for every athlete who came before you and every young athlete watching you now. For the first time in NCAA history, college athletes have the legal right to profit from their name, image, and likeness. That's power. That's progress. And that's pressure.

But here's the truth: this is about more than income. It's about **impact**. You're not just earning — you're learning, shaping your future, and rewriting what it means to be a student-athlete.

You are part of a movement that will be studied, emulated, criticized, and remembered. The decisions you make today, financially and personally, will echo for years to come — in your bank account, your brand, your legacy.

So let's pause and reflect. Look how far you've come.

2. What You've Learned So Far

You've worked through a lot in this book. Let's revisit the key lessons you now carry in your financial playbook:

- **Budgeting**: Like a playbook for your money, helping you call the right plays before the game even starts.

- **Credit**: A score that's more powerful than your stat line. It can open doors or shut them.
- **Banking**: Choosing the right accounts and understanding fees, access, and digital tools.
- **Taxes**: Knowing what Uncle Sam expects when you get paid through 1099s, cash, or collectives.
- **Investing**: Getting your money to work as hard as you do — slowly, consistently, and strategically.
- **Business formation**: LLCs, EINs, contracts, agents — making your NIL game a professional enterprise.
- **Branding**: Understanding your unique story, positioning yourself on and off the field, and showing the world who you are — not just what you do.

But above all, you've learned this: **Financial literacy is not a one-time lesson. It's a lifelong practice.**

3. The Real Game Is Life After Sports

No matter how far your athletic journey takes you — whether to the pros, to a corporate office, or to a business of your own — one day the uniform comes off. When that happens, what remains?

Answer: **Your financial habits.**

Every NIL dollar you earn is a down payment on your future self. Are you stacking it or spending it? Building with it or blowing it? Are you making moves your future self will be proud of?

The average pro career is short. Injuries happen. Coaches change. Fans forget. But your financial foundation? That's forever.

Let's talk about what that foundation looks like.

4. Stacking Your Wins: Building a Life Beyond NIL

Think of your NIL journey like a season. You had your training camp (learning the ropes), your regular season (earning money, managing deals), and now — it's playoff time. Can you turn short-term wins into long-term wealth?

Here's how:

a. Automate Your Growth

Set up automatic transfers from your checking account to savings and investing accounts. You won't miss what you don't see. Pay yourself first.

b. Diversify Your Hustle

NIL is a stream of income. You'll need **multiple streams** to build wealth: business ventures, investments, royalties, brand partnerships, digital content, real estate. Start with one. Build from there.

c. Invest in Your Mindset

Wealth isn't just money. It's knowledge, relationships, discipline. Read books. Find mentors. Stay coachable. Evolve.

d. Live Below Your NIL Level

Just because you can flex doesn't mean you should. Remember: the loudest one in the room is often the brokest.

e. Legacy Over Likes

The likes fade. The highlight reels age. Focus on impact. What can you build that your kids, your community, and your people can benefit from?

5. The Power of "No"

A major part of financial maturity is **saying no** — to distractions, bad deals, clout-chasing, and sometimes even family or friends.

When you earn money, people see you as the bank. It's not your job to be the savior. It's your job to build something strong enough to take care of you — and eventually, to give back without going broke.

Saying "no" doesn't mean you don't love them.

It means you love your future more.

6. Who You Have Around You Matters

You need a team off the field as solid as the one on the field. Surround yourself with:

- A **financial advisor** who understands student-athletes and your goals.
- A **CPA** who knows NIL taxation and can keep you legal and compliant.
- An **attorney** who reads the contracts before you sign them.
- A **mentor** who's been where you want to go — or farther.

Cut anyone who doesn't respect your boundaries or your vision. Protect your peace and your paper.

7. Your Brand Is Bigger Than a Logo

NIL is about identity. It's about how the world sees you — and how you see yourself.

When you're intentional about your brand, you attract the right partnerships, create trust, and build a platform that can outlive your athletic career.

You don't need 100,000 followers. You need **alignment**. Be real. Be consistent. Be strategic.

Own your story — because if you don't, someone else will tell it for you.

8. Generational Wealth Starts Now

You might be the first in your family to earn this kind of money at this age. That makes you **a pioneer.**

Use this opportunity not just to change your life — but your whole family's trajectory. Here's what that looks like:

- Open investment accounts.
- Set up emergency savings.
- Avoid predatory lending and debt traps.
- Educate your siblings and friends.
- Protect your assets with insurance.
- Start talking about legacy: wills, estate plans, and giving back.

Your NIL dollars have the power to plant seeds your grandchildren can harvest.

9. From NIL to CEO

You are the CEO of *You, Inc.*. Whether you go pro in sports or something else, NIL is your first taste of being in control of your brand, your business, and your future.

Don't waste it.

- Track your expenses like a CFO.
- Make vision boards like a creative director.
- Invest wisely like a venture capitalist.

- Network like an executive.
- And protect your peace like a CEO who knows their worth.

Even when you're broke, act like the boss you're becoming.

10. The Culture Needs This

You're not just doing this for you.

If you're a first-gen college athlete, a young Black or Brown student, an athlete from a low-income background, an immigrant child, a kid from a small town — you represent something bigger.

Your wins are symbolic.

When you learn to handle NIL money, taxes, branding, contracts, and long-term planning, you're breaking cycles. You're building something new.

The world expects you to fumble this.

Let's prove them wrong — with grace, excellence, and financial savvy.

11. Keep the Conversation Going

Here's the real flex: this book is not the end. It's the **beginning** of your financial literacy journey. Don't stop here.

- Re-read sections as you grow.
- Share this book with teammates and classmates.
- Host NIL literacy workshops at your school.
- Start a YouTube channel, a podcast, or a blog sharing what you learn.
- Connect with me (Pat Brown, MBA) and other professionals who care about your future.

Make financial literacy part of your *lifestyle,* not just a lesson.

12. You Are the Blueprint

You are what we've been waiting for.

The NIL era isn't just a trend — it's a cultural shift. And you are the blueprint. Others will study your moves, mimic your decisions, and model their approach after what you do right now.

That's why it matters.

- Every budget you build is revolutionary.
- Every contract you read is protective.
- Every investment you make is a protest against poverty.
- Every tax form you file is power in motion.

You are changing the game.

13. Final Play: A Checklist for NIL Athletes

Before we close, here's your **NIL Financial Literacy Final Checklist**:

- Budget monthly
- Track your income
- File your taxes (and keep receipts)
- Create a content calendar
- Meet with a financial advisor
- Open a Roth IRA or investment account
- Review your contracts with a lawyer
- Keep personal and business money separate
- Set financial goals: short, mid, and long-term
- Learn one new financial concept every month

If you do these 10 things consistently, you're ahead of 95% of student-athletes — and even most adults.

14. See You at the Top

In closing, I want to say thank you. Not just for reading this book, but for **caring about your future**. That's rare. That's powerful.

I wrote this because I've been where you are. I've seen athletes struggle — and I've seen them thrive. The difference wasn't talent. It was **knowledge, discipline, and guidance.**

So wherever you go from here — the league, the lab, the boardroom, the classroom — carry this with you:

Money doesn't change who you are. It amplifies who you already are.
Learn to manage it now... so it doesn't manage you later.

The world is watching. Your younger self is rooting for you. Your future self is depending on you.

So let's build something that lasts.

I'll see you at the top.

— Pat Brown, MBA

Author. Financial Advisor. Former Student-Athlete. Advocate.

Disclosure & Disclaimer

This book, *Financial Literacy For NIL*, is written with the intent to educate, empower, and encourage student-athletes and those who support them to take control of their financial lives. The information presented throughout these pages is based on the author's personal experiences, professional insights, and research gathered over the course of more than two decades working in financial services, athlete education, and personal development. However, it is critical to understand the following:

This publication is not intended to serve as legal, financial, tax, accounting, or investment advice. It should not be relied upon as a substitute for professional consultation or services from qualified advisors who are licensed to give such guidance.

Educational Purpose Only

All content in this book is presented for general educational and informational purposes only. The purpose is to provide readers—especially student-athletes—with foundational financial concepts, frameworks for responsible decision-making, and awareness of common challenges and opportunities related to Name, Image, and Likeness (NIL).

The content has been prepared to share strategies, ideas, and insights that may help athletes begin to think critically about their financial futures. It is not personalized advice, nor should it be interpreted as a financial roadmap specific to your unique situation.

Everyone's financial, legal, and personal circumstances are different. What works for one student-athlete may not be right—or even safe—for another. Before making any decisions involving money, contracts, legal agreements, or business ventures, it is strongly advised that you consult with the appropriate licensed professional.

No Legal Advice

Although NIL has created new legal territory for student-athletes, this book does not provide legal advice or substitute for the expertise of an attorney. If you are considering signing an NIL agreement, establishing a business entity, reviewing a sponsorship contract, or dealing with intellectual property concerns, it is essential that you consult a licensed attorney who specializes in sports law, entertainment law, or NIL-specific issues.

The laws governing NIL vary by state, institution, and athletic association, and they continue to evolve. It is your responsibility to ensure that you are in compliance with all relevant laws and regulations.

No Financial or Investment Advice

While this book discusses important financial topics such as budgeting, saving, investing, taxes, and wealth-building strategies, it does so from an educational perspective. It is not intended to provide individualized financial advice or investment recommendations.

You should not take any actions based solely on the information in this book without first consulting with a Certified Financial Planner™, licensed financial advisor, or other qualified professional. Decisions about investing, retirement planning, insurance, and tax strategies require personal analysis and should take into account your risk tolerance, financial goals, income, and expenses.

The author does not represent or warrant that any of the strategies discussed will result in a specific outcome or guarantee future financial success.

No Accounting or Tax Advice

This book is not written by a CPA, tax preparer, or enrolled agent. Any references to taxes, deductions, business expenses, or IRS-related topics are based on general understanding and public information and should not be interpreted as tax advice.

Tax laws, filing requirements, and deduction eligibility can vary greatly depending on your status, income, and location. If you are earning NIL income, especially if you're self-employed or managing a business entity, you should seek advice from a licensed tax professional or accountant. Only a qualified tax advisor can help you properly structure your income, determine quarterly tax obligations, and avoid penalties or audit risks.

No Guarantees or Promises

Reading this book does not guarantee any financial gain, NIL success, or long-term wealth creation. Success depends on many factors including personal discipline, decision-making, the quality of your advisors, market conditions, and sometimes—life's unpredictable circumstances.

This book is meant to provide motivation and guidance, not guarantees. Any case studies, examples, or hypothetical scenarios mentioned are for illustration only and do not represent actual outcomes you can expect.

Limitation of Liability

By reading this book, you acknowledge that the author, Pat Brown, MBA, and all affiliated brands or websites—such as FinancialLiteracyForNIL.com, FinancialLiteracyForStudentAthletes.com, FinancialLiteracyForCollegeCoaches.com and others—are not responsible for any decisions you make or outcomes you experience based on the information provided herein.

Neither the author nor any entity mentioned in this book shall be liable for any loss or damage, including but not limited to financial loss, legal issues, tax penalties, or other consequences that result directly or indirectly from your use of the content.

Encouragement to Seek Professional Help

It is the author's firm belief that every student-athlete deserves a qualified support system that includes legal, financial, and academic professionals who understand their unique needs and pressures. This book is intended to complement—not replace—that system.

If you do not currently have a financial advisor, agent, attorney, or tax professional, you are encouraged to begin building a trustworthy team as soon as possible. Making good decisions early can have a profound impact on your long-term future.

Important Tax Dates for NIL

January

- **Jan 1 – New Tax Year Begins**
- Start tracking all NIL income and expenses using a spreadsheet, Google Sheet, or app like QuickBooks or Expensify.
- **Rule of Thumb:** Set aside **25%–30%** of every NIL payment for taxes.
- **Tip:** Keep a separate business checking account just for NIL.
- **Jan 15 – 4th Quarter Estimated Tax Payment Due**
- If you earned more than $1,000 in NIL profits last year and didn't have taxes withheld, you must file this payment.
- **Form to Know:** IRS **Form 1040-ES**
- **Jan 31 – Deadline for Receiving Tax Forms**
- Brands and platforms should send:
- **Form 1099-NEC** (for endorsement or sponsor payments)
- **Form 1099-K** (for payments from platforms like Venmo, PayPal, Cash App—if over $600 in total)
- **W-2** if you had a job on payroll (less common for NIL)
- **Tip:** Store all forms in a digital folder labeled "2024 Taxes – NIL"

February

- **Start Preparing Your Tax Documents**
- Gather all income statements, receipts for expenses (travel, gear, training, media kits, marketing, etc.).
- Track mileage if driving for events or brand appearances.

- **Tax Form Reminder:**
- If you're doing your own taxes, get familiar with:
- **Schedule C (Form 1040)** – to report self-employed NIL income
- **Schedule SE** – to calculate self-employment taxes (15.3%)

March

- **March 15 – Tax Filing Deadline for LLCs or S-Corps**
- If you created a business entity (LLC or S-Corp) for NIL income, this is your filing date.
- **Form to Know: Form 1120S** (for S-Corps)

April

- **April 15 – Major Tax Deadline**
- File your federal income tax return.
- Make your **1st quarter estimated tax payment** for this year.
- Last chance to make contributions to an **IRA** or **HSA** for the previous year (if eligible).
- **Forms to Know:**
- **Form 1040** – Individual Income Tax Return
- **Form 4868** – Extension form if you need more time
- **Tip:** File even if you can't pay—penalties are much higher for not filing than for not paying.

June

- **June 15 – 2nd Quarter Estimated Tax Payment Due**
- Don't forget this if you're self-employed through NIL.
- **Mid-Year Tip:**
- Recalculate estimated taxes if your NIL income is increasing. Adjust your savings plan and consider working with a tax pro.

July

- **July 1 – NIL Anniversary**
- Good time to review contracts, revisit your rates, and assess your financial goals.
- **Money Tip:**
- If you're earning consistently, consider forming an **LLC** to protect yourself legally and potentially unlock new deductions.

September

- **September 15 – 3rd Quarter Estimated Tax Payment Due**
- **Tax Prep Tip:**
- Begin organizing receipts, mileage logs, contracts, and expenses in advance of the busy fall season.

October

- **October 1 – FAFSA Opens**
- NIL income may affect your financial aid eligibility, especially if you're a dependent student.
- **October 15 – Extended Tax Return Deadline**
- If you filed for an extension in April, this is the final day to submit your return.

November

- **Year-End Planning Begins**
- Schedule a meeting with a financial advisor or tax pro.
- Revisit budgets.
- Maximize deductions (buy gear, renew websites, pay for media/training).
- Consider charitable contributions.

- **Rule of Thumb:**
- Track and document **every NIL-related expense**. It reduces your taxable income.

December

- **December 31 – Final Day for Many Tax Moves**
- Last chance to:
- Make business-related purchases
- Contribute to some retirement accounts (SEP IRA or Solo 401(k))
- Book NIL deals that count toward this year's income
- **Tax Tip:**
- Use this time to calculate whether you've met or exceeded the IRS safe harbor rule:
- If you pay 100% of last year's taxes (or 110% if you made over $150k), you'll avoid underpayment penalties.

Bonus: NIL Financial Best Practices

- **Always Save 25%–30% of Each NIL Check for Taxes**
- **Keep Business & Personal Finances Separate**
- **Track All Expenses Related to NIL Work**
- **Get a Pro** – Work with a tax preparer, financial advisor, or CPA who understands NIL and athlete income
- **Review Your State Rules** – Some states tax NIL income differently
- **Use Free Tools** – Google Sheets, QuickBooks Self-Employed, Keeper Tax, MileIQ

Final Word

This book exists because financial education is a powerful tool. It can open doors, protect your legacy, and give you the confidence to take control of your future. But just like in sports, success off the field depends on strategy, teamwork, discipline, and knowing when to call in the experts.

Use this book as a **guide**, not a rule book. Let it inspire action—but not substitute for professional advice. Be curious. Stay informed. And always ask questions before making important decisions.

Need Help? Start Here

Reach out to trusted professionals like:

- *Pat Brown, MBA* – Former D1 athlete, financial literacy advocate, and advisor to student-athletes nationwide.

Contact Info:

Website: www.financialliteracyfornil.com
Email: info@financialliteracyfornil.com
Join our Newsletter to stay updated!

Final Word: Use This. Don't Shelf It.

These tools aren't meant to sit in the back of a binder. Use them. Revisit them. Share them. This is your playbook for life after the game—so stay sharp, stay curious, and keep leveling up.

Definitions and Questions!

Financial Terms

1. **Asset** – Anything you own that has value (cash, stocks, property).
2. **Liability** – Money you owe (debts, loans).
3. **Net Worth** – What you own (assets) minus what you owe (liabilities).
4. **Budget** – A plan for how you spend and save your money.
5. **Emergency Fund** – Money set aside for unexpected expenses.
6. **Compound Interest** – Earning interest on both the money you invest and the interest it earns over time.
7. **Diversification** – Spreading your money across different investments to reduce risk.
8. **Roth IRA** – A retirement account where your money grows tax-free.
9. **Brokerage Account** – An account that lets you buy and sell investments.
10. **ETF (Exchange-Traded Fund)** – A type of investment that holds many stocks or bonds in one package.
11. **Inflation** – The rising cost of goods and services over time.
12. **Credit Score** – A number that shows how trustworthy you are with credit.
13. **Interest Rate** – The cost of borrowing money, or what you earn on savings.
14. **Risk Tolerance** – How comfortable you are with investment ups and downs.
15. **Stock** – A share of ownership in a company.
16. **Bond** – A loan you give to a company or government that pays you

back with interest.

17. **Capital Gain** – Profit made from selling an investment for more than you paid.
18. **Liability Insurance** – Insurance that protects you if you're legally responsible for damage or injury.
19. Term Life Insurance – Life insurance that covers you for a specific time period.
20. Financial Literacy – Understanding how money works so you can make smart decisions.

Accounting Terms

1. **Income** – Money you earn from work, business, or investments.
2. **Expenses** – Money you spend on living or business costs.
3. **Profit** – What's left after you subtract expenses from income.
4. **Loss** – When expenses are more than income.
5. **Cash Flow** – Money moving in and out of your account.
6. **Invoice** – A bill you send when someone owes you for a product or service.
7. **Receipts** – Proof of purchases or expenses.
8. **Write-Off** – An expense you subtract from your income to lower your taxes.
9. **Deduction** – A legal reduction in taxable income.
10. **Depreciation** – The decrease in value of something you own over time.
11. **Revenue** – Total money made before subtracting expenses.
12. **Net Income** – What you keep after taxes and expenses.
13. **Gross Income** – Total money earned before expenses or taxes.
14. **Audit** – A review of your financial records, usually by the IRS.
15. **Chart of Accounts** – A system for organizing financial transactions.
16. **Bookkeeping** – Keeping track of income and expenses.
17. **Taxable Income** – The income you pay taxes on after deductions.
18. **Form 1099** – IRS form that reports income from gigs or NIL deals.

19. Form W-9 – The form brands ask you to fill out before paying you.
20. Schedule C – Tax form used to report business income and expenses.

Agent Terms

1. **Representation Agreement** – The contract between you and your agent.
2. **Commission** – The percentage your agent earns from your deals.
3. **Endorsement Deal** – A paid partnership where you promote a brand.
4. **Exclusivity Clause** – A rule that limits you to working with only one agent or brand.
5. **Conflicts of Interest** – When your agent's personal interest may go against yours.
6. **Negotiation** – The process of working out the best terms in a deal.
7. **Deliverables** – The specific things you must do for a deal (posts, appearances).
8. **Licensing** – Permission for a company to use your name, image, or likeness.
9. **Performance Bonus** – Extra pay based on results (like follower growth or sales).
10. **Term Sheet** – A summary of the major points in a contract.
11. **Appearance Fee** – Payment for showing up at an event or doing media.
12. **Confidentiality Agreement** – A contract to keep information private.
13. **Agent Certification** – Approval by a league or organization to represent athletes.
14. **Legal Counsel** – A lawyer who reviews deals and protects your interests.
15. **Brand Deal** – Agreement to promote a product or service for pay.
16. **Retainer Fee** – Upfront payment to keep an agent or professional on call.
17. **Termination Clause** – Conditions under which you or the agent can end the contract.
18. **Royalty** – Money earned over time from the use of your image or

content.

19. **Scope of Work** – The exact duties and expectations in a deal.
20. **Compensation Package** – The full value of what you're being paid (cash + perks).

NIL Terms

1. **NIL** – Name, Image, and Likeness—the right to profit off your personal brand.
2. **NIL Deal** – Any agreement where you get paid to use your NIL.
3. **Brand Collaboration** – Partnering with a company to promote their products.
4. **Influencer Marketing** – Earning income through social media promotion.
5. **NCAA Guidelines** – Rules that govern NIL activity and eligibility.
6. **Disclosure** – Reporting your NIL deals to your school.
7. **Fair Market Value** – A reasonable payment amount based on your influence.
8. **Boosters** – Donors who support athletic programs (must stay within NIL rules).
9. **Collectives** – Groups that pool money to fund NIL opportunities for athletes.
10. **Content Usage Rights** – Who owns the content you create or appear in.
11. **NIL Compliance** – Making sure your deals follow NCAA and school policies.
12. **Eligibility** – Your ability to keep playing as a student-athlete.
13. **Monetization** – Turning your platform into income.
14. **Brand Ambassador** – A long-term NIL partnership with a brand.
15. **Social Reach** – The number of people who follow or see your content.
16. **Media Kit** – A document that shows your stats, brand, and value to sponsors.
17. **Affiliate Deal** – You earn money based on how many people use your

promo code or link.

18. **IP (Intellectual Property)** – Your content, brand, or image that you own.
19. Pay-for-Play – Illegal under NCAA rules—being paid just to play a sport.
20. NIL Valuation – An estimate of what your NIL brand is worth.

Manager Terms

1. **Business Manager** – A pro who handles your income, expenses, and financial planning.
2. **Brand Strategy** – The plan for how you grow and monetize your personal brand.
3. **Campaign Management** – Overseeing the execution of your sponsorships and content.
4. **Contract Management** – Handling the paperwork and deadlines tied to your deals.
5. **Talent Management** – Representing your overall brand across opportunities.
6. **Publicist** – A manager who controls your public image and media presence.
7. **Scheduling** – Organizing appearances, content drops, and interviews.
8. **Revenue Stream** – A source of income (NIL deals, merch, speaking gigs, etc.).
9. **Client Roster** – The full list of talent a manager represents.
10. **Brand Alignment** – Making sure deals match your values and audience.
11. **Social Strategy** – How and when you post, who you target, and your message.
12. **Deliverable Tracker** – A tool to monitor if you've completed everything in a deal.
13. **KPI (Key Performance Indicator)** – Metrics that show how well your deals perform.

14. **Payout Schedule** – When and how you get paid.
15. **Usage Monitoring** – Making sure your name/image isn't used without permission.
16. **Approval Workflow** – The process for reviewing and approving content or deals.
17. **ROI (Return on Investment)** – Whether your work brings in results for a brand.
18. **Crisis Management** – How to handle bad press or mistakes publicly.
19. **Content Calendar** – Your posting and promotion schedule.
20. **Digital Asset Management** – Organizing your photos, videos, and brand content.

Questions to Ask a Financial Advisor

1. **Do you have experience working with student-athletes or NIL clients?**
   (You want someone who understands the unique challenges and timing of athletic income.)
2. **Are you a fiduciary, and how do you get paid?**
   (Fiduciaries are legally required to act in your best interest. Know if they charge fees, commissions, or both.)
3. **Can you help me create a budget and investment plan for my NIL income?**
   (Make sure they offer both short-term and long-term guidance.)
4. **What's your approach to helping clients build long-term wealth?**
   (This tells you if they're focused on growth, protection, and education.)
5. **How do you help clients plan for taxes, insurance, and unexpected expenses?**
   (Great advisors consider the full picture—not just investing.)

Questions to Ask a CPA (Certified Public Accountant)

1. **Do you have experience with self-employed income or NIL clients?**
   (You need a tax pro who understands 1099s, write-offs, and how NIL fits in.)
2. **Can you help me track and deduct business expenses related to NIL?**
   (They should help you organize your finances and lower your tax bill legally.)
3. **Do you offer quarterly tax planning and estimated payments?**
   (NIL earners often need to pay taxes quarterly—this is critical.)
4. What records and receipts do I need to keep for tax season?(A good CPA helps you stay audit-proof.)
5. Do you offer audit support or representation if I get flagged by the IRS (You want someone who's got your back if things get complicated.)

Questions to Ask an Attorney

1. **Do you have experience reviewing NIL contracts and athlete agreements?**
   (Only work with lawyers who understand the language of NIL.)
2. **Can you explain the risks in this contract or deal in plain terms?**
   (You're hiring them to protect you from what you don't know.)
3. Do I need to trademark my name or brand? Can you help with that?(You may need legal protection for logos, slogans, or digital content.)What are the legal consequences if I break a contract—or if the brand does?(Know your rights and liabilities before signing anything.)
4. Can you help me set up a business entity like an LLC?
   (Many student-athletes need this for tax and legal protection.)

Questions to Ask an NIL Manager

1. **What services do you provide outside of helping me get deals?**
   (Good NIL managers help with brand strategy, scheduling, and long-term planning.)
2. **How do you choose which brands or partnerships are a fit for me?**
   (You want someone who's looking out for your image—not just quick cash.)
3. **How do you get paid—and do you take a cut from every deal?**
   (Transparency is key. Make sure the pay structure is clear.)
4. Will you help manage content delivery, deadlines, and communication with brands?(They should make your life easier, not harder.)
5. How do you help athletes plan for life after sports and NIL?
   (The best managers think beyond today's deal and into your future career.)

Questions to Ask an NIL Agent

1. **Are you certified to represent student-athletes for NIL deals?**
   (Some states, schools, or organizations require certification or registration.)
2. **What brands or clients have you worked with before?**
   (Look for experience that shows they can deliver results.)
3. **Do you negotiate contracts yourself or bring in legal/financial professionals?**
   (An agent should work with your full team—not replace them.)
4. How do you protect my rights in a deal, and what happens if things go wrong?
   (A good agent should protect you as much as promote you.)
5. What's your long-term strategy for helping me grow my brand and income?
   (The goal isn't just more deals—it's smart deals that build your future.)

5 Questions to Ask Alumni Who Could Help You Later

1. **What was your transition like after college or athletics?** *(Great for hearing real stories about life after the game and gaining perspective.)*
2. **What advice would you give someone in my position who wants to succeed beyond sports?** *(Shows respect and opens the door for mentorship.)*
3. **How did you build your career or business after graduation?** *(Learn from their journey—and possibly find opportunities to follow.)*
4. Are there any organizations, events, or people you think I should connect with? (Tap into their network—you might be one introduction away from a big opportunity.)
5. Would you be open to staying in touch or mentoring me as I start planning my future? (This respectful ask shows you're serious—and opens the door to long-term connection.)

Questions to Ask Potential Business Partners

These questions will help you determine if someone is a good fit for collaboration and long-term success.

1. **What are your long-term goals for this business or project?** *(Make sure your visions align before joining forces.)*
2. **What strengths do you bring to the table—and what do you expect from me?** *(Clarity on roles prevents resentment or confusion down the road.)*
3. **How do you handle conflict or disagreements in a team setting?** *(Conflict will happen—it's how they handle it that matters.)*
4. **Are you financially invested and prepared to handle early-stage ups and downs?***(Money issues are one of the biggest reasons partnerships*

fall apart. Get clear now.)

5. **How will we measure success, and what happens if we want to exit or scale differently?**
   (You need shared expectations and a plan for growth—or even separation—if needed.)

About the Author

***Pat Brown, MBA** is a former Division I football player turned financial educator, advisor, and fierce advocate for student-athletes navigating the new world of Name, Image, and Likeness (NIL). Drawing from both personal experience and professional expertise, Pat brings a unique, authentic voice to financial literacy—one that speaks directly to athletes who are building brands, managing income, and preparing for life after the game.*

After playing football at the University of Kansas, where he served as a team captain and competed at the highest level of collegiate athletics, Pat briefly played in the CFL before turning his focus to the business world. Motivated by the financial struggles he witnessed among teammates, peers, and even in his own family, Pat earned his MBA and dedicated his life to helping others make smarter money moves.

Over the past 20 years, he's worked as a wealth advisor, insurance specialist, and financial literacy speaker—educating student-athletes, parents, and professionals on topics like budgeting, credit, investing, taxes, entrepreneurship, and building generational wealth.

*Pat is the founder of **FinancialLiteracyForNIL.com**, a platform designed to empower student-athletes with tools, curriculum, and real-world knowledge for managing NIL income wisely. He also works with universities, high schools, athletic departments, and community organizations nationwide, helping athletes see themselves not just as competitors—but as CEOs of their own brand and future.*

A husband, father, and lifelong learner, Pat believes that the game may end—but the lessons, habits, and impact you build through financial literacy last forever.

Yes, if you print this off I will sign it....your welcome!

Yes, I will also sign this picture as well if you print if off..

Made in United States
North Haven, CT
10 November 2026

22084525R00153